Stories from the Front
By Lt. Jeffrey J. Coonjohn
Copyright © 1991 by Jeffrey J. Coonjohn

Library of Congress Catalog Card Number: 91-93100

ISBN: 0-9631199-0-7

The Military Press
P.O. Box 26594
Fresno, CA   93729-6594

Printed in the U.S.A.

Dedication

To my wife Heidi, who struggled through medical school and took care of our wonderful children while their daddy was at war.

Acknowledgement

Without the assistance of Col. Jack Horak ("Brass Tacks Jack"), my experiences with the Army would have been dramatically different. I extend my sincere thanks to Col. Horak for his invaluable help in making my experiences what they were.

Notes

Where it is relevant, I have referred to instances before the initiation of hostilities as Operation Desert Shield and after the commencement of hostilities as Operation Desert Storm. When my intent is to capture the entire event, I refer to Operation Desert S/Storm.

There are no international standards for spelling Arabic names. In fact, driving between Dammam and KKMC, I saw the city of Hafar Al Batin spelled three different ways on English road signs. I have adopted spellings used in military or U.S. government publications although these are not officially adopted spellings.

Finally, in some instances I have combined several events into one incident for easier reading. In so doing, I may have overlooked individual contributions that are due recognition. These events are based upon my recollections, however, and while I can't claim it is without error, it is a fundamentally accurate account of my life at The Badger Pit.

The army taught me some great lessons--to be prepared for catastrophe--to endure being bored--and to know that however fine a fellow I thought myself in my usual routine there were other situations in which I was inferior to men that I might have looked down upon had not experience taught me to look up.

--Oliver Wendell Holmes, Jr.

CONTENTS

Operation Desert Shield

Shortly after Iraq invaded Iran in the fall of 1980, the six governments on the Arabian Peninsula established the Gulf Cooperation Council (GCC). The sovereign countries of Kuwait, Bahrain, Oman, Qatar, Saudi Arabia and the United Arab Emirates (UAE) sought to enhance military preparedness by providing a "shield" over the peninsula. The apparent concern of the GCC was that the Iranian fundamentalist government of Ayatollah Khomeini might be successful in its war with Iraq, thus posing a significant threat to the other gulf states. In fact, Iran had asserted territorial rights to Bahrain and its animosity toward the west would not bode well for the pro-western countries of Kuwait and Qatar. Iraq's claims against Kuwait, which dated back to the last century, were not considered threatening despite numerous incidents and border skirmishes over the years. In 1973, Iraq had even occupied the Kuwait border post of Al Samitah.

In 1983, with no mind toward the Iraqi claims, troops from all GCC member states participated in an exercise called Shield of the Peninsula. Military commanders hailed the exercise as a success and the following year carried out another maneuver called Shield of the Peninsula II. The second exercise was held in Saudi Arabia at King Khalid Military City (KKMC) near Hafar Al Batin, eventually to become the hub of Operation Desert Storm. The GCC concept of providing a shield over the peninsula was incorporated by the U.S.-led Coalition, thus the name Operation Desert Shield.

There were 34 countries that comprised the shield over Saudi Arabia. These were known as Coalition Forces. In addition, the Soviet Union, Romania and Singapore contributed men and equipment to the effort.

Coalition Countries

Afghanistan	Denmark	Niger	Syria
Argentina	Egypt	Norway	Turkey
Australia	France	Oman	UAE
Austria	Germany	Pakistan	USA
Bahrain	Greece	Poland	
Bangladesh	Italy	Qatar	
Belgium	Kuwait	Saudi Arabia	
Britain	Morocco	Senegal	
Canada	Netherlands	South Korea	
Czechoslovakia	New Zealand	Spain	

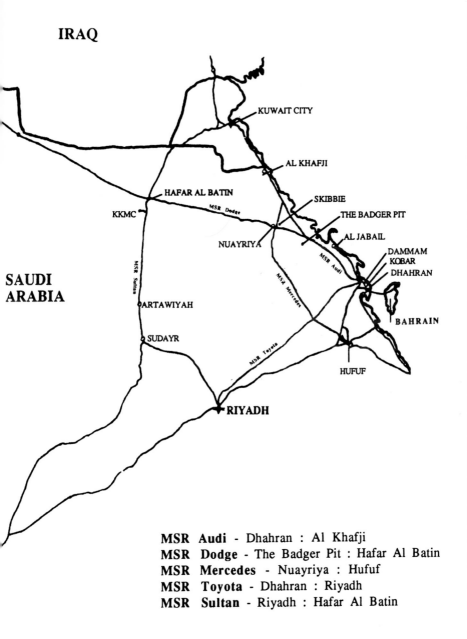

IRAQ

KUWAIT CITY

AL KHAFJI

HAFAR AL BATIN

SKIBBIE

KKMC

THE BADGER PIT

MSR Dodge

AL JABAIL

NUAYRIYA

DAMMAM
KOBAR
DHAHRAN

MSR Audi

SAUDI
ARABIA

MSR Safwa

MSR Mercedes

BAHRAIN

QARTAWIYAH

SUDAYR

MSR Toyota

HUFUF

RIYADH

MSR **Audi** - Dhahran : Al Khafji
MSR **Dodge** - The Badger Pit : Hafar Al Batin
MSR **Mercedes** - Nuayriya : Hufuf
MSR **Toyota** - Dhahran : Riyadh
MSR **Sultan** - Riyadh : Hafar Al Batin

Introduction

"All rise." Justice Heffernan of the Wisconsin Supreme Court entered the court and sat down. After three arduous years of law school I was about to be sworn into the State Bar. On the judges cue, I raised my right hand and repeated the oath. "I, Jeffrey J. Coonjohn, do solemnly swear. . . ." After I finished the oath, I stepped forward and signed in the book of attorneys: "Date of Entry, August 21, 1990." Even though the whole process took less than an hour, I didn't feel as though I needed more. Law school had been a grueling experience for me. Throughout, I had worked two jobs, had two children, completed an ROTC program, completed Army Airborne training and helped my wife through her first three years of medical school. She had only nine more months until completion.

More than the shock of standing before the highest court in the state as one of its officers, I felt a sense of relief at having completed what I assumed would be the hardest part of my life. I picked up my two daughters from the baby sitter and took them to the park. Katie, who was now 18 months, was ecstatic about spending the afternoon with her daddy. Neither my wife Heidi nor I had been able to spend many weekdays with the kids. Between work and homework, our schedules had been saturated. Only on the weekends could we put everything aside and devote the entire day to some family outing. Hilary was a little less than two months old so she was less effected by our restricted time.

Katie and I played most of the day at the park. We took turns pushing Hilary's stroller through the zoo and we chased the ducks around the lake shore. When we got home, Heidi was studying. Together, she and I fed and bathed the kids before putting them down for the night. After the kids were asleep, I turned on the television to watch the evening news.

Over the last two weeks all the news reports were centered around the Middle East. On August 2, 1990, Iraq had invaded Kuwait. President Bush had publicly condemned the invasion and indicated that the Iraqi action compromised U. S. security interests. Saddam Hussein, Iraq's self-appointed leader, ignored President Bush's warnings. The president responded by sending a number of troops to the region. Although I had been commissioned in the Army for just over a year, I didn't feel in any danger of being called up out of the reserves.

Shortly after ten p.m., the phone rang.
"Do you have your bags packed, Lt. Coonjohn?" I recognized Col. Horak's booming, gruff voice.
"Excuse me, Sir." I needed a minute to digest what he was saying.
"We don't have the orders yet," he said, "but it looks like you've won an all expense paid vacation to Saudi Arabia." He laughed at his joke. We talked for a few minutes longer. I told him that I would be at the Reserve Center first thing in the morning. I didn't say anything to Heidi.

When I entered the office the next morning, SSG Lindy Weinman-Bong was already at her desk. She was working on a charity fund raiser that was supposed to take place the following month. Our unit was raising money for the Special Olympics. Lindy was also the Unit Administrator and knew most of what was going on.

"What's happening?" I asked her.

"We're being activated," she said. "We're going somewhere in the Middle East. The news is all over 4th Army and I think even our group knows." We were a company, our headquarters was a battalion and their headquarters was known as an Area Support Group (ASG).

"How sure is it?" I was looking for some shred of hope that after three years, I would finally get some time with my family.

"It's for sure." She said. I knew by the way she answered that she was certain. The Army's Non-Commissioned Officers (NCOs) communicated quite a bit between themselves. She had probably talked to the Command Sergeant Major at the group headquarters.

I didn't say anything more. I went outside into the chilly morning. How many times in how many wars had men felt what I was now feeling? I was proud to serve my country but I was heartbroken at the prospect of being separated from my family. I picked up the kids only an hour after I had dropped them off.

"Are you crying, daddy?" Katie asked me as I put her in the car. The tears were streaming down my face.

Over two weeks elapsed and still no orders were issued. I played with the kids whenever I could but I was now spending at least 12 hours a day at the Reserve Center preparing for the inevitable. Finally, just before midnight on September 15, 1990, the phone rang. I lifted the receiver and the voice on the other end relayed the code words for a national emergency and then began: "By Order of the President of the United States, you are hereby ordered to report...."

After he finished, I hung up the phone and sat in the darkness. This was it, I was going to war. I called my mother in Alaska. I told her the news and asked if she could come and stay with Heidi and the kids for a month or so. She readily agreed. Although my step-father was from Wisconsin, most of my family lived in Alaska which is where I was born.

Within a week, I was at Fort McCoy, WI. My only concern now was coordinating the movement of soldiers and equipment 10,000 miles across the world to a sand-covered kingdom called Saudi Arabia.

The Expo and Beyond

More than half the troops deployed to Saudi Arabia under Operation Desert S/Storm spent a night or two at a holding area near Dhahran: Cement City, The Port, Khobar Towers, etc.. For me and the other members of the 826th Ordnance Company from Madison, Wisconsin, the holding area was the Dhahran Exposition Center, called The Expo. Some stayed only a few days at these holding areas, while others stayed months. For most, it was an introduction to Saudi Arabia.

The Expo had long ago filled to sleeping capacity when we arrived on November 12, 1990. It was headquarters for the 593d ASG, several battalions and scores of companies. Our company, like most of the three thousand soldiers housed at The Expo, slept in tents surrounding the green and turquoise building. The crowding and eventual overcrowding of the facility, resulted in lines being formed for everything. There were lines for the five public telephones from which monitored calls could be placed to the United States. These calls were limited to five minutes and cost over fifteen dollars apiece. There were

1

lines for the Post Exchange Store (PX) that was operated by volunteers seeking some relief from the boredom. There were lines for the chow hall that catered an Arabic interpretation of American food. There were lines for the filthy outdoor showers that only had cold water--when they had any water at all. And, there were lines for the toilets that consisted of no more than small barrels parked below strips of plywood, usually infested with sand flies. Fortunately, my unit was one of the lucky few who spent only a short week at The Expo before being sent north toward the Iraq/Kuwait border. When we left The Expo for the last time, it was with relief and recognition that in the open desert there would at least be relative privacy!

The Dhahran Exposition Center (The Expo) was used as a holding area for American troops deployed to Saudi Arabia.

During our stay at The Expo, there were no organized activities and very little to do. Writing letters consumed most of the hours although some people played volleyball or baseball. Everyone started a diary. Most afternoons there were practice gas warfare drills which consisted of wearing a gas mask for half an hour or so. On Wednesdays, the drills lasted up to two hours. After a couple days at the Expo, I plotted to get out. I felt claustrophobic on the few acres of sand to which we had been fixed. Escaping from The Expo wasn't as difficult a chore as I had anticipated. I stood on the road by the only exit route and flagged down vehicles to see where they were going. After no more than twenty-minutes, I hitched a ride with a couple of guys going to the Dhahran airport on a mail run. We passed by the gate guards with ease and I felt as though I was free again. The two mail clerks knew their route fairly well and pointed out highlights along the road: Sports City, Souks Supermarket, Toyland, Khobar and the Dhahran International Hotel. It had been six weeks since I'd had a non-military meal, so I opted to get off at the hotel. The truck dropped me at the curb about a half block from the entrance. I surveyed the area before continuing. The hotel was a lavish green oasis amid otherwise barren terrain. Irrigation fed trees, shrubs and even the greatest luxury--grass! I grabbed hold of my gas mask which had become my constant companion and strapped my M-16A1 over my back. With some trepidation that I might appear out-of-place wearing my BDUs (Battle Dress Uniform), I approached the door to this five star hotel. As I entered, I found that the hotel served as headquarters for the Joint Information Bureau (JIB). The JIB was composed of the ministries of information from various Arab states as well as the American military Public Affairs Office (PAO). The much maligned media pools that so rankled the press, originated at the JIB. Media pools were nothing more than military escorted tours to selected sites. Travel outside of the media pools was severely limited.

With the exception of my rifle, I melded in with the soldiers working at the military PAO. To the right of the tile entry were the hotel registration desk and service center. The service center included an overseas information area and an exchange where dollars could be converted to

Saudi riyals. For each American dollar exchanged, you received 3.75 Saudi riyals. There were also six public telephones from which international telephone calls could be placed. Not all telephones in Saudi Arabia could be used to dial internationally. Public telephones had either "NATIONAL," in green lettering or "INTERNATIONAL," in blue lettering across the top. The Dhahran International Hotel boasted all blue telephones. Directly to my right, between the revolving door and the service desk, a corridor entered into a small shopping mall. Most of the stores had been taken over by the media who had converged on the hotel in order to better cover the crisis. A travel agency and British Airways still thrived, however. To the left was an identical corridor with some very fine shops: a specialty bakery, a florist, a gift shop, a newsstand and a dry cleaners. Except for during legally mandated prayer times, the shops remained open. Directly in front of me was a comfortable lounge and talking area. As there were no bars in Saudi Arabia, the lounge was a popular meeting area.[1] From the second floor, a beautiful chandelier hung down so that the mezzanine had a loft-type appearance to it. Cigarette smoke from the lounge swirled upward enveloping the crystal lights in a hazy fog. Beyond the lounge was a restaurant. I walked through the lounge, entered the restaurant and sat down. Despite the declining sophistication of its clientele, the restaurant hadn't changed its gourmet menu. Where two months earlier Arab sheiks ordered famous foreign meals, I now ordered a good old fashioned hamburger and a Pepsi.[2] Compared to the food we had been getting at The Expo, it was terrific.

After my meal, I spotted a large man surveying the restaurant. He stood nearly 6'3" and weighed about 250 pounds. His hair was greased back and his baggy suit made him appear as though he had just emerged from a 1950's drama.

---

[1] Islamic law forbids the consumption of alcohol, therefore, it is outlawed in many Muslim countries.

[2] Because it operated a bottling plant in Israel, Coca-Cola products were banned from Saudi Arabia until just recently. Although now available, Pepsi still dominated the market.

The Dhahran International Hotel in Saudi Arabia. Headquarters for the Joint Information Bureau (JIB).

He carried a lit cigarette although I never saw him smoke. Something about him reminded me of Perry Mason. He caught sight of me watching him. He smiled broadly and walked over to my table with his hand extended. "Good afternoon, my friend!" His voice was almost booming. Reflexively, I put out my hand and introduced myself. He bowed as we shook hands and proceeded to rattle off some long unpronounceable name. Seeing my puzzled look, he laughed. "Everyone calls me 'Sammy,'" he said. Sammy's accent seemed Indian although his complexion was more Western. He managed the Dhahran International Hotel for its Arab owners. Sitting there with Sammy in the din of the restaurant with smoke swirling about the lights, I felt as though I was part of an unfolding drama. The atmosphere seemed drawn from a spy movie. I wondered if CIA, KGB and MI-6 men were lurking about under the guise of correspondent or entrepreneur. Sammy didn't seem the spy type. He was more interested in American baseball. Had I ever been to a baseball game? Had I ever seen Nolan Ryan pitch? What did Americans think of Sadaharu Oh, the Japanese home run king? I wasn't much help to

8

him. Although I loved the sport, I hadn't followed it in years. Still, we had a good visit. Sammy bought my lunch and beckoned me to follow him. By the service desk he pointed to a phone. "Call home," he said. "It's on the house." It was easy to see how Sammy was so well connected. He read people and did his best to please them. He was as much a part of the character of the hotel as the blue arches that surrounded it. I called my wife for the third time in as many days. I missed her and I missed the kids. I made a second call to my friend Joel De Spain, who worked for WISC-TV in Madison. I let him know that we had arrived safely and that everyone was well. I promised to keep him informed on how the Wisconsin units were faring throughout the war.

Sammy was speaking Arabic to several Saudi businessmen so I didn't bother him. I bought an English language newspaper at the newsstand and I left the cool air conditioning of the hotel. The temperature outside was near 100 degrees. I glanced at the headline on the newspaper. President Bush had chosen not to rotate troops in the Gulf. It looked as though I was going to be there for a while. On September 21st, Saddam Hussein had promised to fight the "mother of all battles" if the Coalition tried to free Kuwait by force. The American build-up had now reached 250,000 soldiers and it looked like force was exactly what the president was planning. Unless Hussein withdrew his troops, we were going to have to fight the "mother" to free Kuwait. Four American jet fighters blasted over the hotel. The earth shook below me. I knew it wouldn't be too much longer before the whole world would shake in Iraq.

In the hotel parking lot, I stopped to talk to a couple of reporters. As we chatted, they mentioned that they were on their way to Khobar. I asked to join them. They were going to the American Corner to do some shopping. The American Corner was about fifteen minutes from the hotel and was popular with journalists. It was also popular with the GIs because it was a place to get a taste of home: Kentucky Fried Chicken, Baskin Robbins and Safeway. On the drive there, my stereotypic views of Middle Eastern cities crumbled. Khobar was a small international city. Besides the franchises at the American Corner, it touted such American businesses as Hardy's, Sizzler, Sears and Budget Rental Cars. But Khobar, like all of Saudi Arabia, also retained some of its provincialism. The mosque was still the center of life and everything was weighed for its religious significance.[3] There was no separation between religion and government.

Just before reaching the American Corner, the reporters stopped at a fast food restaurant called Med Mac's. The restaurant had an identical logo as McDonald's and promised the menu of the international giant. According to the two reporters, however, the food was atrocious! Utilizing the McDonald's logo without being affiliated with the corporation was a blatant breach of international trademark law. When we arrived at the American Corner, I found that the restaurant's trademark infringement was not an anomaly. New music releases were being sold for far below American retail prices. For

---

[3] A mosque is an Islamic temple. It is easily recognized by the crescent moon that appears over its domes.

two or three dollars you could by the latest American hit cassette tape. With a little investigation, I found that the tapes were pirated copies made in the United Arab Emirates. Intrigued by these flagrant breaches of international law, I decided to seek out a lawyer and find out more about Saudi Arabia's legal system. I had, after all, been graduated from law school only a few weeks before my call to active duty. I bid the two reporters goodbye and walked up the Coastal Road toward Khobar's central district.

Med Mac's restaurant had an identical logo as McDonald's but without delivering the taste or quality of the international giant.

The American Corner with a Safeway grocery store, Baskin Robins ice cream parlor and Kentucky Fried Chicken.

الرجاء
(عدم جلوس النساء بالمحل)
(حسب تعليمات هيئة الامر بالمعروف)
الاداره

PLEASE
AS PER THE LAW
LADIES ARE NOT ALLOWED
TO SIT IN THE PARLOUR

Woman were not allowed to sit in the ice cream parlor or in restaurants--except in designated locations.

Until that very day my knowledge of Islamic Law was confined to quips about "an eye for an eye." I never really considered the concept of Islamic Law as a jurisprudential system. I was in for a surprise.

With a few directions from some locals, I located a nondescript building on the perimeter of the central district. Its facade of white stucco looked like so many other buildings and its arched, smoked windows so common, that I first mistook the building for a residence. Only the small wooden sign on the fence identified the law practice of Abdul Mohammed Sieed.

Mr. Sieed, like many practicing attorneys in Saudi Arabia, was a man well schooled in the triad that forms the basis of Islamic Law. The Saudi legal system, known as the *sharia*, draws upon *The Koran*, the words of Mohammed and the traditional works of religious scholars for its sustenance. In Islam, law and religion are one. There is no formal code as Westerners know it and precedent holds no major legal significance. Despite this, the criminal justice system has surprising continuity, probably because *The*

Koran speaks so clearly to criminal misconduct. In civil law, however, the *sharia* becomes almost completely ineffective. Business decisions and contracts need to be based upon an exactitude that Islamic law cannot provide. For that reason, investment in Saudi Arabia is extremely speculative. The payoff is often so great, however, that most businesses find it worth the risk.

Perhaps it was because I was carrying an M-16A1 and 120 rounds of ammunition, but I had no trouble getting an immediate appointment to see Mr. Sieed. I vowed to try the technique the next time I had an appointment with an American attorney. Mr. Sieed was quiet, courteous and very patient. He spoke fluent English, French and Arabic. We talked for a short time about comparative legal systems and especially about the *sharia*. Islamic law, he explained, deals swiftly and mercilessly with the crimes of theft, rape, adultery and murder. Rehabilitation plays no part in the *sharia*. A petty thief, for example, may incur a long prison term or the payment of heavy reparations. More egregious thieves, however, may find themselves sentenced to public amputation of their right hands! These public punishments are carried out in an almost ritualistic atmosphere. An excited crowd pushes and vies for position. Then, a government executioner, wielding a specialized sword, delivers the punishment. The bloody dismembered limb, still reflexively grasping, falls to the ground. A string is then tied to one finger and the dripping hand is hoisted up a pole or hung off a balcony for all to witness. This public display exacts a community revenge and seeks to show that justice has been served. Whether or not such bloody displays are effective is uncertain, but Saudi Arabia does have one of the lowest crime rates of any country on earth.

For rapists, adulterers and murderers, justice wears a similar veil. Once convicted, a murderer or a rapist finds himself at the mercy of the victim's family. While public beheading is the custom, the victim's family may choose to forego the execution and accept a large money payment instead. This is the derivation of the term, "blood money." More often, the victim's family chooses public beheading. Not all these punishments are carried out by the government, however. If public execution is the family's choice, then the family may choose to administer it! Whereas the government's executioner is a professional whose swift sword falls but once, family executions may result in the murderer being hacked to death before chanting crowds. The images evoked by the public carving of another human is repugnant to most Westerners: decapitated heads rolling about attempting to speak, severed veins spewing blood as the heart pumps out its life, or dismembered hands reflexively reaching out. No matter how vile foreigners may think Arab justice, it is an integral part of a nearly fifteen hundred year-old religious tradition.

Inflicting capital punishment for adultery is unique to Islam in the modern world. While early American settlers once branded or ostracized adulterers, under the *sharia* they suffer the same fate as rapists or murderers. That is, their families are publicly dishonored and the adulterer is decapitated. Because infidelity must be proven beyond any doubt, the public execution of adulterers is very rare.

There has been only one in the last twenty-five years. In accordance with Islam's male dominated society, female adulterers suffer an even worse death than their male counterparts. Once the crime is confessed or proved beyond any doubt, the female adulterer is bound and drawn before a great wall. A forebodingly quiet crowd circles around her. Brandishing rocks and stones they await the executioner's signal. Thus given, the crowd attacks like frenzied shark amid a pool of blood. Through chants and jeers and a hail of stone, the unfaithful woman is bashed until dead! The uncontrolled crowd is then dispersed by police indiscriminately clubbing whomever is unfortunate to be within their reach. During Operation Desert S/Storm, while the world's eyes were fixed on Saudi Arabia, the Kingdom, ever vigilant of its international image, executed no public punishments.

The next few days at The Expo were spent organizing additional duty assignments and preparing for our move north. Our company commander (C.O.) was Stanley R. Berg. He participated very little in the command structure. The way the military is designed, the officers are supposed to dictate policy, prioritize work and determine overall planning. This, then, is given to the senior NCOs, whose job it is to ensure that the plans are carried out. The junior enlisted do the actual physical work. Unfortunately, this was not the way our company worked. Our C.O.--"Stanley" we called him--was a computer genius. From the day of his call to active duty, to the day of his release, his mind revolved around either appropriating, operating or programming computers. Stanley was the type of guy who probably wore a slide ruler and white socks in college. He was too nice and too eager to please to effectively command. This created a leadership void at the top. The officers were torn between an allegiance toward military protocol and getting the job done. Therefore, the void was inappropriately filled by the First Sergeant, Lon Kaderavek. Lon, in effect, ran the company. It was a confusing state of affairs, especially for the officers. No one was truly happy with the situation but because our senior NCOs had at least twenty-years experience each, they made it work. The result was that the officers received their orders from battalion and operated only within their respective duty positions, leaving the First Sergeant to control the overall operation. While this structure allowed the unit to complete its mission, it did not always provide for harmonious living. Lon occasionally made decisions against which the officers revolted by pressing the commander to exert his authority. In all fairness, it was not comfortable for Lon either.

One of the additional duty assignments to which I was assigned was supply officer. I was now a platoon leader, in charge of operating the first magazine platoon; the supply officer; the legal affairs officer; the personnel officer; and the Class B Agent, in charge of all cash funds within the company. One of my duties, along with my two good friends Chief Warrant Officer Dennis Stone (Stoney) and Warrant Officer Terry Hackett (Hackman), was to ensure that life in the desert would be as comfortable as possible for the troops. Like myself, Stoney and Hackman were dedicated to making the best of a bad situation. Their dedication to their soldiers probably resulted from their experiences in the Vietnam conflict. In Vietnam, they both had felt a nonchalance from their officers that they were determined not to convey in this war. Despite the similarity of their objective, Stoney and Hackman were almost completely opposite in their demeanor. Stoney, who stood only 5'2" in combat boots and two pair of socks, was very easy going, never rushed and never allowed himself to be rushed. He lived without regard for the clock. When he was tired, he slept. When he awoke, he got up--it didn't matter that it might be three a.m.! His jovial attitude never betrayed his 44 years. Stoney also enjoyed practical jokes, although sometimes they were a little macabre. When confronted with the gnarled death and destruction of the Iraqi army in northern Kuwait, Stoney took out a bumper sticker that he had brought from home and placed it on an enemy tank. It read: "Escape to Wisconsin!"

Hackman, on the other hand, derived his nickname from the combination "Wildman Hackett." He was an interesting sort of guy. Always in some activity, he never seemed to stop. He was hyperactive and humorous but always suspicious that Iraqi infiltrators lurked behind every Arab cloak. Hackman was always concerned about his soldiers, however. He successfully integrated the Army maxim; "Mission first, soldiers always!"

I tried to stay somewhere in the middle between Hackman and Stoney. While I wasn't that concerned about military regulations or customs, I did work feverishly to accomplish whatever mission I was assigned. Like Stoney and Hackman, everyone called me by my nickname-- LT.

Together, we three troopers became companions and friends, dedicated toward making the best out of whatever we were given. Once we received our mission, we realized just how big a task that was going to be. Our assignment landed us in the middle of the desert--110 miles north of Dhahran and 110 miles nearer the Iraq/Kuwait border. The only thing in our vicinity was a rock pit dug out of the hard desert floor. After only six days in Saudi Arabia, we were ordered to the pit. We named it The Badger Pit, after our own Wisconsin Badgers.

Warrant Officer Terry L. Hackett (Hackman)

Chief Warrant Officer Dennis Stone (Stoney)

The Badger Pit.

24

THE CRAPPER CAPER

Almost immediately upon our arrival at The Badger Pit, a very critical need arose. The closest outhouse to our work area was more than a quarter mile away. This was a problem for two reasons. First, when drinking nine quarts of water per day, as the Army recommended, frequent relief was necessary. This was not too difficult a problem, however, as most soldiers simply relieved themselves whenever and wherever the urge struck. The primary problem was that most digestive tracts were still growing accustomed to the morning T-trays served by the mess section. Morning T-trays consisted of green powdered eggs, packaged cereal and eight ounces of irradiated milk.[4] When the T-trays first appeared, they were a welcomed sight. Previously, our meals had consisted of an Army invention known as Meals Ready to Eat or MREs. MREs consisted of a main dish such as pork and beans, barbecued beef or spaghetti; a dessert, such as freeze dried pears or chocolate nut cake;

---

[4] Irradiated milk is specially treated to last months without refrigeration.

and crackers with either cheese, peanut butter or jelly. Each ingredient was hermetically-sealed in heavy plastic and placed in a dark brown bag. When the average daytime temperature was over 100 degrees, the MREs took on a taste and texture unique even for military food.

The intestinal adjustment from MREs to T-trays provided for many a queer gait over the quarter mile journey between the work area and the outhouse. A few track records were probably even set as people sought not to soil their already unclean uniforms. The situation soon became desperate and action was necessary. We determined that an outhouse in the work area was the only answer. While this might sound like an easy construction job, you must remember that wood is a very scarce commodity in the desert and not something to be wasted on such luxuries as an outhouse. This left us with limited alternatives. As always our first step was to check the military supply channels. CPT Ginni Bradford, who was my supply boss at battalion, investigated and found that the "Portable Human Feces Relief Stations" were a contract item backordered for thirty to forty-five days. This seemed somewhat at odds with what I had observed at Al Jabail Port. The sailors and Marines at the port appeared to have an abundance of outhouses spread throughout each pier. It was obvious to me that our need for an outhouse and the Navy's abundance of outhouses was a distribution problem crying to be resolved. So, with a little planning, I decided to redistribute a "Naval Contemplation Station" to The Badger Pit.

There were two possible means of attack. One, drive into the port in broad daylight and load the outhouse onto a 5-ton truck and drive away; or operate with stealth and acquire the mission objective on a night raid! Both plans presented problems. In daylight, the person responsible for the stations would clearly see seven Army soldiers attempting to load an outhouse onto an Army vehicle. Similarly, the nighttime raid also would be doomed because of the strict security at the port. We were, after all, preparing to go to war! The solution was to combine the two plans. We would drive into the port at three a.m. and load up an outhouse as though we were on an assigned mission from some higher headquarters.

On the morning of 30 November 1990 at two a.m. we departed The Badger Pit to accomplish logistical redistribution for "rear area support." My driver, as always, was SGT Jeff Crum of Wisconsin Dells. With us in the Blazer were Specialist Roger Repta ("Reptile"), Specialist Dan Freed and Specialist Brent Friedl. We were followed closely by Specialist Shawn Keiner and Specialist Mike Lynch ("Vern"), who was driving his 5-ton truck. We bounced and bumped over the three mile desert road leading from The Badger Pit to the six lane Main Supply Route known as MSR Audi. All but two of the major roads in Saudi Arabia were code named after automobiles. There was MSR Dodge, MSR Yugo, MSR Buick, MSR Audi, MSR Mercedes, MSR Toyota and the exceptions MSR Sultan and MSR Yankee. Our location at The Badger Pit was just before the MSR Audi/MSR Dodge junction. During the forty-five minute drive to Jabail, I turned on the radio to catch up on the news. Both Armed Forces Radio and the BBC came in better at night. It had been an eventful day. For the first time, the United Nations voted to forcefully evict Iraq from Kuwait if they didn't withdraw by January 15, 1991. President Bush now had his "high noon" deadline. Even though that deadline was still forty-five days away, the prospect of war loomed larger than it ever had. Hussein was still vowing to fight!

With our military IDs we had little trouble negotiating the gate guards and the security checkpoint going into Jabail Port. At pier 18 we spotted our first series of relief stations, ten little white houses lined one next to the other. We pulled up next to the outhouses and immediately realized that a nature stop was in the offing. Opening the spring loaded door, I was struck not so much by the offensive odor that burst out like an explosive blast, but by the fact that these military facilities were actually stocked with toilet paper! The white gold of desert warfare! In short order, we successfully relieved ourselves of fluid and the Navy of its seemingly endless supply of toilet paper. The mission was then at hand. Utilizing a night vision scope, I scanned our vicinity looking for any potential deterrents. None spotted, we went to work. We dropped the sides to the 5-ton and began to hoist an outhouse into the bed of the truck. The sloshing and jostling of the structure caused us to move faster. In turn, the faster we moved the more sloshing occurred, until our hands were wet with urine-laced water. I couldn't help but break the silence with laughter. Soon all seven of us were frantically trying to rid ourselves of the outhouse while laughing hysterically at our filthy predicament. The higher the outhouse rose into the air, the more unsteady she became until, losing all control, she slammed backwards into the bed of the truck. Vern, whose truck was now being soaked with whatever was contained in the reservoir, yelled out in his slow midwestern drawl: "My truck! Look at my truck! It's covered with. . ." As the words were leaving his mouth a large, wet pile of human excrement floated down the bed of the truck, over the side and onto Vern's foot. While the rest of us rolled with laughter, Vern stood silently looking at his boot. I then noticed that our attempt at stealth had failed dismally. Several Marines assigned to guard the ammunition, had been drawn by our clamorous caper. Amused by Vern's situation, however, they said nothing and we successfully strapped down the load and went back to our place in the sand.

The Post Exchange

As we continued to settle in at The Badger Pit, I learned from Ray Black of the Army and Air Force Exchange Service (AAFES), that with the proper documentation our company could set up a small field exchange, selling items like those that might be found at a convenience store. This non-profit store would be funded by AAFES as a service to GIs in the Gulf. On December 6th, I received the paperwork. It was on that day that Saddam Hussein announced that he would release the foreign hostages he had been using as human shields. Within eight days, all the hostages would be home. On December 7th, 1990 (Pearl Harbor Day) I received a $12,000 credit from AAFES. I could now purchase stock from their warehouse to supply our company PX. Because ours was the first company level PX in Saudi Arabia, we were treated equally with exchanges that grossed more than a million dollars a month. It was without too much difficulty that I convinced Ray that we needed a cash register, a calculator, shelving and miscellaneous display items. We received nearly everything we asked for with the all important exceptions of a microwave oven and a refrigerator. I ordered these through the Army system, although I was skeptical whether we would ever receive them given the dismal condition of American supply operations. The next problem was trying to find an adequate facility from which to operate our PX. There were no fixed buildings in the desert, so we would have to acquire a structure that would be mobile and one that would be available through supply channels. The only solution seemed to be to utilize a large, military tent. I scavenged through the war stocks held by the 321st MMC, and soon had a new store and an ideal place to live.[5] With the C.O.'s incessant questioning about computers, the Officer's Tent was becoming increasingly uncomfortable for me. So, with Stoney and Hackman, I moved into the back of the new PX tent while the store was moved into the front. Vern, who had recovered from our crapper caper, and SPC Leo Endres, were set to work building an interior for the tent. With lumber we salvaged from the Port of Jabail, they put in a wood floor and framed walls. They then

---

[5]Materiel Management Center

covered the walls with ten sheets of paneling that I mooched from some Filipino construction workers in Dhahran. Soon we had Arabic prayer rugs on the floor and 3' x 5' posters on the wall. The Badger Pit was beginning to build a reputation as an American desert oasis.

Operating a convenience store in the middle of the Saudi Arabian desert, was more difficult than I think most of the soldiers realized. Inventory was the primary problem. First, our reputation had grown such that units from all over the area were shopping at our store. This demand created an enormous restocking problem. Even the Brits, whose palates are markedly different from Americans, found something at our PX. Every night after our eight o'clock close, I would get Stoney or SGT Crum and after searching for a vehicle, we would make the two hour journey to Khobar. There was nearly always a problem getting a vehicle. The unit had two types of passenger trucks: pickups and Blazers. While I was assigned a Blazer on paper, it was usually needed for the ammunition operations, or so I was told. In any case, there was nearly always a tussle for transportation. Everyone wanted something, but no one wanted to give-up their vehicle. When we did finally get a vehicle, we would usually go to the local outdoor market (called a souq) where we spent one or two thousand dollars on local purchases. Then we would shop at the 24-hour American Safeway or Souks Supermarket, often spending an additional three thousand dollars a night. It was not unusual for us to return to The Badger Pit at three or four in the morning. Sleep was a luxury that·we could not afford during these first few months if we were to accomplish our objectives. Between the PX warehouse and our local purchasing, the variety and popularity of our inventory soared. We carried everything from Hostess snacks to the daily English language newspaper, the *Arab News*. We carried T-shirts, shoe polish and Arab prayer rugs, ash trays, film and even an edited version of *Time* magazine.[6] We sold Saudi and Kuwaiti flags and operated a VCR tape rental service! Eventually, I was even

---

[6] While Saudi Arabia allowed the sale of American magazines, it edited each and every magazine before it was sold. The editors removed or defaced advertisements or pictures that did not comport to Islamic standards. They would even withhold an entire issue if there was something adverse about Saudi Arabia in the content.

able to establish Flower Fax and film processing centers so that soldiers could send flowers anywhere in the world for as little as $25.00 or send developed pictures back to America--all from a green, sand-covered tent in the middle of the desert!

PX manager SSG Steve Marek open and ready for business!

The size and complexity of the PX operation and its logistics grew exponentially. It was increasingly difficult to operate the PX and adequately perform my other duties. Fortunately, SSG Steve Marek came to the rescue. Steve was the unit movement coordinator whose job was to handle logistics during transit.

Since we had arrived at The Badger Pit and weren't likely to be moving, however, Steve found himself without much to do. Steve was "volunteered" by the First Sergeant to work at the PX. From his first day on the job, he managed the store as well as any supermarket chain manager. It was often a thankless job. Every night saw a another struggle for a vehicle and every day saw more complaints about what we didn't have or how expensive our stock was, even though our prices were identical to Exchanges in the United States. Steve handled it superbly and with the help of two great workers, SPC Jeffrey Radloff and SPC Shari Heiser, the operation flowed smoothly. When our ammunition operations slowed down, there was a joke that went around the company to the effect that the only ones in the Army with full-time jobs were the PX workers and the outhouse cleaners. At The Badger Pit this was probably true--at least until the Army contracted a sanitation company to clean the outhouses. When we acquired additional ammunition operations further north, I opened a branch PX. The smaller size of the branch operation allowed us to utilize a metal container van (conex) for our operations.

SPC Eugene Kidd, who had worked at The Badger Pit PX, became the branch manager. In a space smaller than an apartment kitchen, SPC Kidd completed sales exceeding $5,000.00 per month!

PX worker SPC Jeff Radloff poses with SPC Byron Bishop.

Souks Supermarket in Khobar.

The Interior of the Badger Pit Post Exchange.

The Post Exchange carried everything from Hostess snacks to English language newspapers.

The AAFES PX warehouse in Dammam also operated as a distribution station for corporate donations. Some of the donations I wrangled from the warehouse included writing cards, water bottles, sun tan lotion and the ever popular, non-alcoholic beer. The initial allocation of NA beer from AAFES was for one beer per person per month. For a unit from Wisconsin (the state with the largest beer consumption per capita in the United States), this was wholly inadequate. I pleaded with Ray and several other workers at the PX warehouse to increase our allocation. For days they listened with deaf ears to my pleas for an increased allocation. Even though I had a good rapport with them and we often exchanged information and rumors, I still couldn't get them to increase our allotment. Every day that I had business in Dhahran, I would stop in at the PX warehouse. By the end of the week, Ray was tired of seeing me. He was in desperate need of wooden pallets that he used to keep food stock off the ground. He proposed to give me 100 cases (1 pallet) of beer for every truck load of pallets I could deliver. I felt as though I had won a major victory and went searching for pallets. I remembered having seen two enormous stacks of pallets in the area. One at the port and the second at a nearby industrial site. About two miles from the PX warehouse, I found the mountain of pallets still stacked next to the industrial complex. I drove through the entrance and discovered that the complex was part of the Colgate-Palmolive worldwide operations. It was Friday, a Muslim holy day, so no one was working except the foreign management teams. I located the manager, who was an American, and asked if we might be able to have some of the thousands of pallets stacked outside. He agreed to give us whatever we wanted and by the time we left the Colgate-Palmolive plant, our every whim had been fulfilled. We had cases of shampoo, toothpaste and soap, enough for everyone in the unit. We had hundreds of blue barrels that could be used for road barriers or who knows what. The *coup de grace*, however, were ten large truckloads of pallets--good for 24,000 cans of beer! I radioed to The Badger Pit for several large trucks. Ray was dumbfounded as the pallets began to arrive on the very day that we had made our agreement. He made good his end of the bargain. It took two forklifts almost thirty-

five minutes to load up the tractor-trailer with
all the beer.   It would all be gone in three
months time.

Marines from Delta 2/24 shopping at the PX.   The
Marines used our showers, dayroom and exercise
facilities when they stopped by our "American Desert
Oasis."

Although it was a substantial amount of work, operating the only company level PX in Saudi Arabia did provide me with some opportunities. The demand for local purchase items like rugs, clothes and traditional Arab garb required continuous local purchasing. This meant anticipating demand then scouring the souqs along the coastal cities of Jabail, Qatif, Dammam and Khobar for bargains. The marketplace or souq is the primary trade center of every Arab town. It is comprised of open stalls, one next to the other, in which merchants deal their wares. "Deal" was the name-of-the-game, too! Items in nearly every store were outlandishly priced, although this was no reflection on what you eventually paid. Every sale was the culmination of offers and counter-offers. These merchants were shrewd businessmen and you had to be prepared to walk away. Overeagerness was an expensive passion in the souq. Within the souq, there were sub-souqs such as the textile souq where colorful cloth was sold, or the gold souq where fine jewelry could be purchased. All merchants of similar wares stayed within their own souq which often resulted in beautiful displays: store after store of gold chains, necklaces and bracelets perhaps followed by the shoe souq with miles of aisles of boots, thongs, tennis shoes, and loafers. There were also sub-souqs for carpet, housewares, food, perfume, watches, clothes, and much more. Adding to the quaint beauty of the souq, were the dazzling fluorescent lights that illuminated the streets with an artificial daylight. Many GIs enjoyed shopping in the souq while listening to the local banter and eating shawarma. Like hamburgers and fries in the United States, Saudi's favorite junk food was the Turkish shawarma. The closest thing America has to offer is the chicken fajita, but that really doesn't do justice to the hot, fresh shawarma. It is made from chicken stacked on a skewer and cooked before an open flame. As the outside of the chicken browns, it is trimmed and placed inside pita bread with parsley, tomato, pepper, onion, lettuce and Tabasco sauce. The result is a handheld feast that rivals the American hot dog. With a little time, anyone can prepare a shawarma. I asked several street venders and through a combination of sign language and my broken Arabic, determined that the best way to prepare shawarma was to marinate two pounds of chicken or thinly sliced beef overnight in the following sauce:

3 or 4 cloves of garlic-minced
1/2 tsp black pepper
1/2 tsp hot pepper sauce
1 tbls finely minced onion
1/2 tsp ground mace

1/2 tsp salt
1 cup plain yogurt
1 tbls vinegar
1/2 tsp red pepper
2 tbls lemon juice

Place the marinated meat in a barbecue rack and cook over hot coals until finished to taste. Combine taheeni, clove of garlic, lemon juice and parsley until creamy; add water if necessary.[7] Place the barbecued meat, sliced tomato, onion, chopped parsley, lettuce and green pepper in a pita bread and pour on the taheeni mixture as desired; sprinkle with Tabasco sauce and you have a shawarma.

---

[7] Taheeni is a paste made from roasted sesame oil and lemon juice. It is emulsified and has a consistency somewhat resembling mayonnaise. Although distributed worldwide, it may be difficult to acquire in some locations--check with a Middle Eastern restaurant or a specialty food store.

The local Shawarma man prepares for the next order.

One of the unique features about the souq was its business hours. Closed through the mornings and afternoons, the souqs opened around four p.m. and remained open until nearly midnight! These late hours proved to be a great convenience for replacing PX inventory and for getting one of our much coveted vehicles. Although this was the middle of December, within two months the Saudis would begin celebrating the holy month of Ramadan. Ramadan commemorates the time when the Prophet Mohammed first received God's revelations. Muslims recognize it as a time to test their reverence so they do not eat, drink or smoke during daylight hours. Most Muslims sleep and pray during Ramadan. After sunset, they break the fast with great feasts and celebrations. Only after the evening feast would the stores reopen. During Operation Desert S/Storm, Ramadan extended from February 17th to March 17th and the stores did not open until eight or nine p.m., but they stayed open until two the next morning! In December, we had to be satisfied with a midnight closing.

The local souq with its unusual business hours: four p.m. to midnight.

Much of the local purchasing for the PX was done at the Khobar and Dammam souqs because their larger size afforded us a greater selection. Often I would buy fifty or a hundred prayer rugs (a big seller in the PX) and argue incessantly over a few Saudi riyals--less than a dollar. The argument was more to show negotiation prowess than over money. A shrewd negotiator was respected among the merchants and received the best quality at the lowest prices. I don't think they'd run into too many American lawyers but believe me when I tell you that there is no experience in the world like haggling with a fervent Arab merchant!

In particular, I remember one vender at the Dammam souq who utilized a unique approach to negotiating a sale. We had argued for some time over the price of flags that I wanted to buy for the PX. Eventually, he agreed to sell me fifty flags at thirty-two riyals apiece--about eight dollars and sixty cents each. I gave him five hundred American dollars and awaited my change. The total cost had only been four hundred and thirty dollars. When merchants made change in Saudi Arabia, it was customary to pay only in paper bills and give some item such as a candy bar or gum in lieu of coin change. For example, if a customer purchased an item for 3.5 riyals and paid with a 5 riyal note, the merchant would give him one riyal change and a pack of gum or a candy bar. Because the value of one riyal was only about twenty-seven cents, not too many Americans took exception with this practice. In this instance, the vender wanted to give me an additional seven flags in lieu of my seventy dollars change! This price was $1.40 more than I had just paid! I pointed this out and another heated debate arose until I consented to take eight more flags and an Arabic prayer rug instead of my seventy dollars.

The Saudi Arabian Flag (green with white inscription).
The inscription reads "There is no God but Allah,
Mohammed is the Prophet of Allah."

Mileage   Chart

	Badger Pit	Skibbie
Badger Pit	0	50
Skibbie	50	0
Jabail	35	85
Dammam	110	160
KKMC *	550	600
Riyadh *	350	400
Madison, WI	9,250 miles	
* southern route		

51

THE ROAD TO RIYADH. . . AND BACK

In the second week of December, we received a message that we were going to be redeployed to King Khalid Military City (KKMC) falling under the 70th Ordnance Battalion and the 226th ASG. The lead time--six days--was extremely short notice to move a company of two hundred people and one hundred pieces of equipment 250 miles, so immediate action was necessary. Coordinating with Hackman, we determined that we would leave The Badger Pit the following morning. Our plan called for us to meet with our new group representatives in Dhahran and then proceed to Riyadh where we would overnight. The following day we would drive north to KKMC. While the purpose of our trip was ostensibly to coordinate logistical support for the unit--food, fuel, water, etc.--we viewed this as the perfect pretext to see Saudi Arabia's much touted capital.

The next morning at four a.m., Hackman and I were on the road south. Anytime Hackman was behind the wheel, it was an experience. After bumping along our desert road, we finally reached the hard-surfaced route leading to Dhahran. Terry romped down on the accelerator. The speedometer needle jumped past 85 mph--the indicator's maximum. For the next hour and a half it never dipped into an area registering on the dash. In the military, the highest ranking person in the vehicle gets the speeding ticket, whether or not he is driving. This is because he has the authority to order a reduction in speed. I ordered such a reduction but Terry's response was not substantial enough for the needle to fall below the red line. I gave up on my protests and instead devoted my attention to watching for the Military Police. In short order, we reached Dhahran. Our new group was located at ARCENT, near the Dhahran International Airport.[8]   After a light breakfast at the airport mess hall, we located our new group. They had received no official notification of our redeployment, therefore, they had not prepared for our move.

---

[8]ARCENT (Army Central Command) was divided into ARCENT Main, located in Riyadh and ARCENT Dhahran. All references are to ARCENT Dhahran unless otherwise stated.

On several occasions, it crossed my mind that the Army's confusion was a planned ruse to confuse the enemy. During these delusions, I imagined that someone, somewhere really had a master plan. After four years in the Army, including Basic Training, Advanced Individual Training, Officer Training, and Airborne school, I knew this was not the case. Since the days of Hannibal, the armies of the world have employed the *management by crisis* technique and the United States had perfected it.[9] Ill-at-ease with our first stop, Hackman and I were back on the road. Again the speedometer needle was buried in the red. With white lines going by so fast that they almost appeared solid, we made the two hundred and fifty mile trip from Dhahran to Riyadh in three hours and ten minutes, an 80 mile an hour average!

---

[9] American officer training programs teach planning with the 7 P's ("Proper Prior Planning Prevents Piss Poor Performance). Everyone realizes, however, that no plan survives intact any contact with the enemy--or implementation for that matter. Proper planning simply allows options to remain open when worst case scenarios prove accurate.

Driving through Saudi Arabia was much like driving through any western country, with two significant exceptions. First, the Islamic religion requires five precisely timed prayer periods throughout the day: preceding sunrise (fajr), midday (dohr), late afternoon (aser), sunset (maghrib) and nightfall (esha). These times change by a few minutes each day based upon the sun's rise and set. For ardent Moslems it matters little in what activity they may be engaged, when the faithful are called, it is time to pray! So, nearing midday on the road to Riyadh, hundreds of cars pulled on to the shoulder of the road, their occupants got out and, facing Mecca, they knelt to pray. These prayer stops also accounted for the second anomaly on the road to Riyadh. Like drivers anywhere, Saudis hated to stop once they got out on the open road. This was probably because it was difficult to bring their vehicles, that they drove at better than 100 mph, to a stop. In any case, many Saudis, making efficient use of their religious breaks, relieved themselves immediately after prayer. While it may not be so unusual to see several hundred people peeing on the side of the road at any one time (although I had never seen it before), it was somewhat unusual from the American perspective to see several hundred men squatting to pee! Americans, especially GIs have no qualms about urinating wherever and whenever the urge strikes. Most American males, however, stand upright and attempt to destroy ant hills or chase insects across the open ground with their hot, fluid streams. Middle Eastern men, on the other hand, squat like perched birds. This difference makes for quite a scene. In order to urinate from the squatting position, a man must expose his buttocks either by pulling down his pants or by lifting his thobe or dishdasha if he is in Middle Eastern attire. Therefore, on the road to Riyadh we saw several hundred men on their knees praying. Then, exposing their rear quarters to those of us so irreverent enough to continue driving, they squatted and relieved themselves--all the time, facing toward Mecca!

Muslims stopping to pray on the side of the road.

Prayer Times

Wednesday	Makkah	Madinah	Riyadh	Dammam	Tabuk	Jizan
Fajr (Dawn)	5:25	5:26	4:58	4:44	5:38	5:13
Dhuhr (Noon)	12:34	12:34	12:06	11:52	12:47	12:23
Asr (Afternoon)	3:54	3:54	3:26	3:11	4:04	3:44
Maghrib (Sunset)	6:25	6:24	5:55	5:40	6:33	6:17
Isha (Night)	7:55	7:54	7:25	7:10	8:03	7:47

The posted prayer times in the *Arab News.*

Although there were many fine, expensive hotels in Riyadh, Hackman suggested that we seek out an American Air Force facility to spend the night. First, they would be free and second, the Air Force had a reputation for comfort among the armed services. Hackman had served in the Navy during Vietnam and had spent additional time in the Army, so I heeded his suggestion. The Air Force motto, he told me, was: "Sleep late, grow your hair long, eat well and aim high." The Army motto was just as simple: "I should have joined the Air Force!"

When we finally found the American Air Force base, we immediately quoted the Army motto. Unlike our tents and cold showers, they lived in barracks resembling a Motel 6, although not as Spartan. Their facilities included an outdoor pool, an outdoor theater, a weight room, game room, 24-hour mess hall and hot showers! We decided that our best approach to wrestle an accommodation from these fortunate warriors would be to seek-out my counterpart in the supply section. The supply officer, CPT Weigand, was more than helpful. He gave us a room, with real beds, clean linen and free phones to call back to the United States. I believe he almost felt sorry for us. We were quite a sight to someone who hadn't been in the field--our clothes were filthy, our hair was grubby and we had a generally dirty appearance. After a warm meal, a warm shower and a phone call to my wife, I felt and looked rejuvenated. That night I enjoyed the best night's sleep I'd had since entering this desert sand.

The next morning we arose just after six a.m.. We showered again--simply because it was available--and went to mess. Very few people were in the chow hall. I asked one of the KPs who told me the mess hall got busy between eight and nine, after people had a chance to shower and enjoy a cup of coffee in their rooms. I was convinced that the Air Force must fall under the Federal Aviation Administration and not the Defense Department because this was surely not how the Army worked! After breakfast, Hackman and I walked around the area. The Hawk and Patriot missiles silhouetted on the horizon in every direction stood on vigilant guard. These people were soldiers too, they just weren't forced to endure life in the field to accomplish their mission.

At half past eight we woke CPT Weigand and thanked him for his hospitality. He directed us to the petroleum point were we fueled up. We took a small detour through downtown Riyadh. This capital city encapsulated the contrasts of the entire nation. Towering over adobe buildings that dated to past civilizations were huge buildings of a twenty-first century design. The country was in the midst of a cultural revolution. With a continued American presence in the country, it wouldn't be too many more years before the king would be signing his own *Magna Carta* relinquishing power to the people.

The unique architecture in downtown Riyadh.

The King Fahd International Stadium in Riyadh.

After driving north for what seemed an eternity, Hackman and I realized that we had taken the wrong road at Sudayr, about 140 miles north of Riyadh. At this early stage in the military build-up, there were no English signs marking interior roads. We seemed to be on the route to Mecca, the holiest Muslim city. We had both wanted to visit this city of Islamic sacrament, but the one English sign we thus far encountered gave us a clear warning: "Non-Muslims forbidden entrance to Mecca and Medina--severe penalties for violators!". Aware of the harshness of Islamic law, Hackman did not wait for the next turn-around. He had no desire to be publicly carved like a holiday turkey. Without warning he slammed on the brakes and the vehicle slid to a halt. A dividing fence between the east and westbound traffic cutoff our immediate retreat. Classic Hackman driving provided the solution. From the far right lane, Hackman made a screeching U-turn. With the speedometer needle once again flat on the dash, we lunged back into the oncoming traffic. I glanced at Hackman long enough to see his eyes glazed over and a hideous grimace on his flushed face. He looked like he had been touched by *The Shining*. I gripped the dash with my white knuckled hands and cursed his driving ability with every word I could muster. The traffic tore by us at a 200 mph collision speed! Finally, a break in the fence appeared and Hackman entered the ditch at better than 85 mph. As we came out of the embankment, the front wheels left the ground and the truck rode like a bucking bronco. Hackman laughed an almost sinister Vincent Price-type laugh. I was exhausted from the adrenalin rush.

We were in the town of Artawiyah, about half way between Riyadh and KKMC when we decided to stop for lunch. We found a small restaurant nestled behind a fuel station so we put off our planned MRE lunch in favor of the local cuisine. Pulling up to the somewhat dilapidated building, I went in to order. Hackman insisted on waiting in the Blazer. "After all," he said, "any one of these Arabs could be an Iraqi!"

As Hackman waited, I went into the restaurant to order. Saudi restaurants, those outside of the cities anyway, are unlike any in the world. First, they have no menus. You must know what you want when you arrive. I discovered early on that flame roasted chicken was a staple offered by almost all restaurants. The few times I had stopped, I had ordered chicken simply because I knew nothing else. At the Artawiyah truck stop I thought I'd try something different, something with cultural flavor. This left me in quite a predicament. Unable to adequately speak the language and without a menu, I was left to shop for food by moving from table to table assessing each customer's dish. The Saudis found this quite amusing. I couldn't find anything identifiable

63

enough to order, so I pointed to some kind of meat dish and tried to tell the clerk I wanted two servings. My sign language was too similar to the Coalition victory sign, however, so everyone laughed, held up their two finders in a "V" and spoke what little English they knew: "Iraq-Boom!" shouted the clerk making a mushroom cloud with his hands. "Bang! Bang!" an old man with no teeth made a six gun with his finger and shot several people. After several more attempts, I gave up on the authentic cuisine, ordered two roasted chickens and left. Hackman and I ate lunch in the Blazer, safely locked away from the desert sand flies and the Iraqi infiltrators!

After Artawiyah there were no cities until KKMC. Between the two cities the topography changed considerably. The land changed from rolling sand hills and dunes to a flat hard surface. The ground colors varied too, alternating between a rust tone and desert tan. Eventually the two colors melded into a light tan with a rust hue extending out into the horizon. I'm certain that the flat earth theory originated in Saudi Arabia and was carried west. At least I understand why Shaykh Baz, the senior member of Saudi Arabia's religious counsel, continues to this day, to insist that the world is flat![10]

The flat desert that extends as far as the eye can see-- interior Saudi Arabia.

---

[10] Saudi Arabia's religious counsel is known as an *ulama.*

There are certain architectural designs that draw the essence of a city into a symbol: the Eiffel Tower in Paris; Big Ben in London and the Golden Gate Bridge in San Francisco. Similarly, in every Westerner's mind there is an architectural style that symbolizes a fanciful place in the Land of Oz--The Emerald City. To most soldiers, KKMC was "The Emerald City." From the open highway the city was invisibly set over the horizon. As we approached, however, the white domes and blue arches from the central mosque rose off the desert floor, shimmering through the heat mirage which looked like so many pools of water. As the city rose up next to the mosque, so too did numerous smaller mosques of the same shape and appearance rise like sentinels at designated locations around the perimeter. The awe-inspiring magnitude of KKMC derived from its stark contrast to the hot desert environment. In the midst of a land bereft of even scrub brush stood a city of lavish design, colorful landscapes and flowing fountains. The mosque was the center of the culture and the city. Its blue walls were spotted with brilliant red and yellow hanging gardens and before its entrance was a huge fountain of fresh turquoise water.

The central mosque at KKMC.

One of the smaller mosques that stood like sentinels at designated locations around KKMC.

As we pulled around to one of the side buildings, I noticed an American. At this time, KKMC housed only a few of the thousands of American soldiers who would eventually call it "home". As we explored the comparatively unpopulated city, we were excited at the prospect of moving to such a great location. We discovered an Olympic-sized swimming pool, a gymnasium and a five star restaurant, not to mention 24-hour access to telephones. Eventually, we found an information officer who directed us to our new home: Log Base Bravo--in the backyard of KKMC. We would be close enough to see the Emerald City with all its alluring delights, but light years away from its comforts. We drove out to Log Base Bravo and found nothing. The ammunition site was nonexistent. No ammunition had arrived nor had any directives been received indicating when shipments would arrive. The only people in the area were an advance party from the 664th Ordnance Co. who had received notice that they too were to run the ammo dump. With both units under warning orders to redeploy, Terry and I figured there was an Army snafu somewhere in the lines of communication. Little did we know just how large Log Base Bravo would eventually grow. A Log Base (logistical base) is a cluster camp providing general support for military activities in the area. Log Base Bravo and KKMC were becoming the hub of the continuing Coalition build-up. At this time, U.S. troops deployed to Saudi Arabia exceeded 300,000! Even though the White House had extended an invitation to Iraq's Foreign Minister Tarik Aziz to discuss peace, war seemed like an eventuality. When, in the middle of our expedition to KKMC, Iraq postponed any peace talks, we were assured the "mother of all battles" would be fought.

After our exploration through KKMC, Hackman and I drove through Log Base Bravo, locating and coordinating our redeployment. There were only a few support units that were operating at this time but we found the locations from which to draw water, fuel, food and general supplies. With a folder full of notes on who, what, when, where and how, we crawled back into the Blazer for our return trip to The Badger Pit. It was evening when we left KKMC. The now beautifully lit mosques retreated into the quivering horizon as we retraced our path to the main road. When we reached the desolate intersection, Hackman turned the wheel to the north and shot into the dark desert. The night was warm and the windows were down. The breeze felt good in the moonlight.

Hafar Al Batin lay some fifty miles to the north of KKMC. With the road free of traffic and Hackman at the wheel, it took less than forty minutes to make the journey. Hafar Al Batin did not have the striking architecture of Riyadh nor its ambivalence toward the impending war. An eerie feeling came over me as we drove into the central marketplace. The open-air shops were busy but we drew most everyone's attention. People would stop whatever it was they were doing to watch us as we drove slowly through. It was not the same as in the south. The people were somber and seemed to look upon us with fear. Not fear from us, but fear of a war we represented, a fear of death. These people who were so close to the Iraqi boarder saw their own possible deaths in a war that seemed all too lethal, although not a shot had yet been fired. The atmosphere weighed heavily upon both Hackman and myself. The gaunt faces peering out from below the traditional head gear (gutra) looked half dead already. The civilian war toll seemed to already have casualties. We turned east toward Abu Hadryia and back to The Badger Pit. As we sped off into the night, the faces from Hafar Al Batin followed us until we vanished into the swirling sand that had engulfed the night desert.[11]

---

[11] The four hour trip between Hafar Al Batin and The Badger Pit was desolate and uneventful. We arrived just after two a.m.. The next morning we were summoned to see the commander and were informed that our transfer had been canceled. We would be remaining at The Badger Pit, which is where we eventually stayed for our entire eight month tour.

A Day in the Life

The months of December and January saw record rainfalls in the desert. The sun-baked sand of summer grew soft with the moisture. The desert roads turned into muddy quagmires after only a few hours rain. The blistering heat vanished, replaced by a damp chill. It seemed almost like fall. The only benefit from this cool weather was the disappearance of the ever-present sand flies. In order to keep ammunition operations going in The Badger Pit, our equipment worked day and night clearing mud from the supply routes. On one exceptional morning, when I did not have business in Dhahran and the rain was pouring down, Hackman, Stoney and I took a few hours off to run some errands and call home. The closest telephones to The Badger Pit were located at the 197th Infantry headquarters, about twelve miles further into the desert. With Hackman behind the wheel, we moved out into the muddy sand. The number and size of the vehicles that had traversed the sandy trail had created mud holes approaching three feet deep. Whole trucks were buried up to their axles in the muddy holes, as were others who had moved too slowly or stopped. Hackman kept the pedal down. Our rear tires spewed mud everywhere and our windshield had zero visibility. Hackman didn't stop. The vehicle bucked, jumped and skidded but we didn't dare slow. It was fun! When we finally reached the phone center, Hackman parked the vehicle so that we were blocking a 5-ton truck. The theory was that if we got stuck, they would have to move us before they could leave.

The AT&T phone center consisted of four tents with thirty phones per tent. There were always lines. Behind the tents, a huge satellite dish linked the phones directly to a New York operator. The system was designed in Alaska where high-tech, remote communications had been perfected. I saw the monitoring van parked next to the dish and immediately recognized the distinctive yellow and blue Alaska license plates. Having been born and raised in Alaska, I skipped the line and went looking for the monitoring technician. It would be nice to talk to someone from my old home town. I knocked and went inside. Bill Diedrich was on the phone to his wife in Eagle River, Alaska. He hung-up and we exchanged introductions. We talked about hunting and fishing and how much we both missed Alaska. There was little news on the war front. The politicians talked (not unusual) and the military continued preparations. Most soldiers sat in the now wet desert, bored and homesick. Bill was suffering from boredom too. He had read every book his wife had sent and was now begging books from friends. I promised to bring him my copies of *Alaska Magazine*. The staff of *Alaska Magazine*, which covers life in "The Last Frontier," had sent free copies to every Alaska serviceman in the Gulf. Alaskans are a tight-knit group who watch out for their own. After we talked for some time, I knew Hackman and Stoney would probably be waiting, so I said goodbye to Bill and promised to bring the magazines when I returned.

LT and Hackman use bottled water to clean the mud from the windshield.

Bill Diedrich from Eagle River, Alaska who operated the AT&T phone centers. The telephone system was developed by Alascom, Inc., experts in Alaska's bush communications.

Hackman and Stoney were indeed waiting in the truck when I finished talking to Bill. I jumped in and we began our harrowing trek out of the mud. When we reached the paved road, we decided to stop by the local gas station to get the English language *Arab News* for the PX. On the way, we diverted to an American mobile truck stop called CSC Zebra (Convoy Support Center). CSC Zebra was located at the junction of MSR Audi and MSR Dodge, only eight miles from The Badger Pit. Every main supply route in Saudi Arabia had a Combat Support Center. Just as the MSRs were named after cars, the CSCs were named after animals, albeit some of the most obscure creatures on the face of the planet: CSC Folger, CSC Yak, CSC Wombat, etc.[12]. In addition to the basic dining facilities available at each of the CSCs, there was often a mobile kitchen that served short order food. These were known as Wolf Burgers--probably because everyone "wolfed" their hamburgers down. Anyway, the burgers were free and tasted significantly better than any other food served in the Army.

---

[12] Although a sergeant at the 691st Main. Bn. told me that a folger was a bird, I could never find it in my ornithology book.

CSC Folger on MSR Sultan operated by the 691st Maintenance Battalion out of Freemont, N.C.

After the burgers, we drove to the truck stop to pick up some newspapers. The peace talks were continuing but the outlook was bleak. We took the papers back to The Badger Pit in time for the PX's twelve o'clock opening. Stoney went to conduct an inspection on some recently received ammunition and Hackman and I went back to our tent. Several guys were in the day room eating popcorn and watching a video tape. No sooner had we opened our tent flap than our mail clerk delivered a message that directed Hackman and me to the Port of Jabail. Once again we were on the road south.

SPC Jeff Hole, SPC Mike Lynch and SPC Todd Hughes enjoy a movie.

Our Jabail stop took only five minutes. Hackman, whose civilian occupation was as an ammunition expert, had to answer several questions. I simply needed to sign some papers to acknowledge receipt of some computer disks that the C.O. had ordered. When we finished this chore, Hackman and I noticed a huge naval ship moored at the next pier. Hackman suggested we visit the ship and take a tour. It was the USS Mercy, a hospital ship designed with full service facilities. We went on board. The ship was immaculate and the atmosphere very relaxed. Most of the injured on board were from auto accidents or back injuries. The injured strolled the decks or sat in the dining facility talking with each other or with the crew. The dining facility offered a superb buffet. Even though we had already eaten lunch at Wolf Burger, the tantalizing buffet was too great a temptation. They had pizza, spaghetti, sirloin tips, baked potatoes and even green salad! I had three dishes of salad, a plate of spaghetti and a piece of pizza. I believe Hackman doubled me.

The rain had begun anew when we left the port. The day had been relaxed and a good break from the "go-go-go" that filled most days. Hackman and I went back to our tent, and while the rain poured down, I wrote a letter to my wife. I too was homesick.

Christmas Shopping for War Supplies

The 295th General Supply Company, where we received most of our Army issued items, did not have any Christmas specials the day after Thanksgiving. Somewhat depressed, I suspected that the holiday season might pass without celebration. I couldn't have been more mistaken. Returning home one night, I found that Hackman had been hard at work. He had found a small bush near the coast and had set about decorating it. His imagination was virile. He used red, blue, green and yellow condoms as ornaments and toilet paper as tinsel. Finally, he added some candy canes. The result was a sexually allusive tree, fondly named "our f---ing Christmas tree."

Scrub brush decorated with red, blue, green and yellow condoms for ornaments and toilet paper for tinsel.

In the weeks before Christmas, General Pagonis, who coordinated overall logistics for the United States, had put command emphasis on mail delivery. Much to his credit, the packages literally poured in. Greetings and parcels arrived not only from friends and family but also from thousands of Americans whose kindheartedness touched every G.I.. I received a box of magazines, candy and books addressed to "Any Serviceman," as well as hundreds of holiday cards from concerned people back home. One soldier received a package that contained several oranges, a bottle of vodka, a glass tumbler and a swizzle stick. The customs label read: "Contains screwdrivers." Everyone enjoyed the Christmas mail. Unfortunately, this happy state of postal affairs ended shortly after the New Year. The mail again became erratic and infrequent. This was not a great problem for packages containing non-perishable items but for packages containing food stuffs, it was disastrous. On December 14, 1990 my grandmother, leading "The Girls in the Kitchen" at the old folks home in Ketchikan, Alaska, mailed me a five pound box of sugar cookies with hopes of a Christmas delivery. Through January,

February and March the cookies languished on some Middle Eastern port.   Finally, on March 22, 1991--98 days after they had been mailed--I received the partially disintegrated box.   It had been such a delight for these octogenarians who were veterans of the two great wars to be participating in Desert S/Storm, that I felt compelled to do more than write them a letter. On a brightly colored piece of paper, I penciled a verse that I had composed.   I dedicated to it everyone who sent cookies to soldiers.

Cookies From Home
Burned on the edges and crisp inside,
Black on the bottom and dreadfully dry,
This batch is not a baker's prize,
These are cookies from home.

Not tender or moist or perfectly laced,
But broken and crumbled and fairly defaced,
They stick in your throat with an aftertaste,
These are cookies from home.

And although the baker tries his best,
Attacking his dough with zeal and zest,
Still nothing compares with all the rest,
The cookies from home, with love, are best!

With only a week remaining before Christmas, we began to form committees.   SSG Lindy Weinman-Bong volunteered to head-up the

Christmas committee. SPC Heather Holderman was placed in charge of decorations and SPC Jane Conway (Jungle Jane) was in charge of activities. As these preparations were being made, the maintenance section was making preparations of its own. We had acquired over fifty blue plastic barrels at the Colgate-Palmolive plant in Dhahran during our great beer trade. The Esser brothers, Jimmy and Mike, had seen these barrels as the last essential element to their wine fermentation process. Using Kool-Aid for sugar and flavor, they set about the delicate task of wine making. By Christmas, over 100 gallons of Kool-Aid wine had been stored at The Badger Pit. By New Year's Day, it was all gone! Much could be said about the wine--how it was sweeter and darker than syrup or how it poured like molasses. But you'll not find one person who'll say it wasn't the best wine they'd had in Saudi Arabia!

On Christmas Day there was not the customary fight for vehicles. I checked out two trucks, loaded one of them with NA beer and went looking for volunteers. I knew that I was going to miss whatever festivities Jungle Jane had scheduled, but what better day to go "shopping" at logistical storage areas than on Christmas. Through the early months, Stoney asked me on several occasions why I got up between four and five a.m. and went to bed after midnight only to hear how much more we needed and with rarely an appreciative word. But that was the point, we needed "stuff." Whether it was a dozer for doing earthwork or a color TV for relaxing during off hours, we needed support. My praise came from the junior enlisted people who knew that the TVs, the VCRs, the PX, the free NA beer, the free writing cards, the games, the popcorn machine and much more, came from doggedly seeking out new supply channels and just plain hard work. Everyone helped to make The Badger Pit the best equipped and the most accommodating place on the desert floor.

On Christmas Day, it was the guys from the "Whack Shack" that volunteered to help. Each tent at The Badger Pit had a name. There was the Cat House, The Club, the POW tent, the Married Tent, and the Whack Shack to name a few. The Whackers who volunteered for Christmas duty were SPC Steve Williams (Willie), SPC John Dillon

(J.D.), SPC Leo Endres (Woody), SPC Bill Jester (Combat Bill), SPC Tim Hopen (Hopi), SPC Dave Jacobson (Snake) and SPC Erv Wylesky (Rounder). Like Stoney and Hackman, they called me LT. We left The Badger Pit near eight a.m. on Christmas morning and while America was attending midnight mass, we seven marauders struck out on another seek and salvage mission.

SPC Melinda Comers, SPC Christine Campbell and SPC Heather Holderman pose in front of the The Cat House -- one of the many tents at The Badger Pit.

Even though it was Christmas, the gas warfare training continued.

Enjoying the winter sports--sand sledding!

Christmas festivities at The Badger Pit.

Our first stop was the 403d Transportation holding center near the Dhahran International Airport. Everyone knew it as it was identified by the entrance sign: "Ghost Town." I'm not sure how the name derived but I assume it was because all unclaimed, unmarked and frustrated cargo ended there. If an item was undeliverable because its markings were missing or incorrect, it went to Ghost Town's cargo warehouse until it was claimed or placed back into war stocks. It usually took three to four weeks to be placed back into stocks, so it was customary to simply claim items that your unit needed.

As we pulled into Ghost Town, it became evident that every company had planned some festivities. The 403d was in the midst of barbecuing and organizing a frisbee contest. Back at The Badger Pit, Jungle Jane had organized a tug-o-war contest between our company and elements of the 197th Infantry Battalion. Our company won three out of three pulls! Jane had also organized volleyball, horseshoes and basketball tournaments. The highlight of the day, however, was the parade. There were numerous creative entries but the

197th took top prize with an armored personnel carrier decorated like Santa's sleigh and eight GIs dressed as reindeer yoked to the forward gun. Although we were a hundred miles into the desert and 10,000 miles from home, the spirit of family between all the service people was evident.

No one was working at the Ghost Town warehouse when we arrived. A few guards were roving about but most everyone was enjoying the activities. A junior enlisted female was on desk duty near the entry. She was dressed in a scanty tank top and shorts. As I approached the office door, she stepped out into the sun. She was blond, very shapely with long slender legs. Her nickname was "Dusty." I talked to her for several minutes more than I probably should have but I successfully received her permission to "look" through the warehouse for some of our "missing" items. Once inside the frustrated cargo area, we loaded-up the vehicle with supplies: leather gloves for the ammunition handlers, nails, hammers and screws for the service section, a holster for the C.O. and miscellaneous truck parts for the maintenance section. I was beginning to get the Christmas spirit! In one corner, I spotted three large, unmarked crates. Willie and Rounder pulled one apart to reveal a true treasure: a satellite dish. We loaded the boxes weighing 750 pounds each into the back of the pickup. I went to talk to Dusty to hasten our departure. Willie and Rounder pulled around the corner a few minutes later. The load was completely covered, with the exception of several shovel handles sticking out the back. "Well," I said to Dusty, "I guess we'll have to check back another time." The smoke from our struggling diesel engine blew by us. The bed of the truck nearly rested on the tires. She smiled and looked me straight in the eye. Neither one of us spoke for several seconds. The sun glistened off her dark, tan body. It had been three months since I had been called to duty. "Come again," she whispered suggestively. I winked. "Merry Christmas!" I said. I jumped in the waiting truck and made a tactical withdrawal. I saw her reflection in the side mirror as we pulled away. She stood smiling and watching us until we made it through the gate, then she turned   and   went   back   inside.

The Whackers from the Whack Shack.

Our second stop that day was at King Abdul Aziz Port. Some weeks prior, on another mission at the port, I had found a small chicken stand operated by Sri Lankan workers. As most American establishments were closed for the day, I decided to treat the Whackers to lunch. We each ordered hot chicken, pita bread and a Pepsi and went outside to eat in the warm December sun. The Persian Gulf or Arabian Gulf as the Saudis called it, was bright turquoise.[13] Unlike the dark greens and blues of the northern

---

[13]Until 1935 Iran was known as Persia, thus the Persian Gulf. For Saudi Arabia and other Gulf states who had territorial and political disputes in the region, the name was unacceptable.

Pacific or Atlantic Oceans, the Gulf was more akin to the Caribbean with its pastel colors. We sat silently for nearly an hour. Combat Bill, Hopi and J.D. called home from a nearby phone. It really didn't seem like we were almost at war. Occasionally, a conversation would flare-up about whether Saddam would withdraw his troops or whether we would be home before our 180 day orders expired. Mostly we just sat, each person reflecting on his own thoughts--mostly of home.

After lunch we drove over to The Expo to see the supply people at the 80th Ordnance Battalion. We drove through tent city and around the back of the main building. I was glad we didn't live here anymore. I got out of the truck and walked toward the back entrance. The company commander of a quartermaster unit was pacing near the entry. I struck up a short conversation with her. She was concerned that her unit had just been ordered to Log Base Alpha near Hafar Al Batin. I reassured her that it wasn't as dangerous as she believed. Although I had been there several times, there was no convincing her. She was certain that she would meet her demise in the Saudi desert. Rhetorically, she mused that if she only had a flack jacket (similar to a bulletproof vest) she would feel much safer. I asked her how many flack jackets she needed. Her face lit up. She said that all she needed were two medium-sized jackets and that she would fill a requisition for eighty sheets of plywood if I could get them for her. We had already resolved our immediate wood shortage at The Badger Pit by scavenging dunnage from cargo ships arriving into Jabail. But plywood was a highly prized commodity in the barren countries of the Middle East and it could always be put to good use. I told her to stand fast and went through a hole cut into the security fence at the back of The Expo. My supply friends from the 80th, SGT Bill Ingersol and SSG Mitch Hayner, were tanning themselves war zone style. They had on boots, underwear and an open flack jacket. Their Kevlar helmets and BDU pants were within a hands reach. Bill and Mitch lived behind The Expo in a maintenance tent converted to storage that they called "Bill's Bar and Grill." I asked Bill about flack jackets. He could get two immediately if the price were right. I offered him ten cases of NA beer and before I could get it delivered from my truck, I had two medium sized flack jackets. I went back to The Expo where the company commander was waiting patiently. As I walked up to her, I thought she was going to kiss me she looked so happy. I handed her the jackets and produced a Materials Release Order (MRO) that I conveniently carried with me. She signed it. The unit now had eighty sheets of plywood. It wouldn't be long before our NCO Corps would have the finest warm water showers possible built at The Badger Pit.

SPC John Williams, SGT Bill Ingersol, Lt. Jeffrey Coonjohn and CPT Ginni Bradford standing outside "Bill's Bar & Grill."

As I was about to go through the hole in the back fence, I heard someone calling my name. It was CPT Ginni Bradford, my boss and the person from whom all regular supply channel items derived. She told me that my request for an 84 cubic foot refrigerator had been denied but that a 42 cubic foot refrigerator would be available for my pick up within the next five days. Our microwave would be ready too! She seemed almost apologetic about the refrigerator but I smiled and assured her that it was a success. Our PX would now have cold drinks, milk, cheese, bread and even yogurt! The Badger Pit was living up to its reputation as an American desert oasis!

We sat at Bill's, telling jokes and stories, mostly just trying to forget that we were so far from home. Although my youngest daughter, Hilary, was celebrating her first Christmas without her daddy, my now two year old daughter, Katie, was the most effected. Katie had begun having nightmares and waking my wife in the middle of the night asking: "Where's Daddy." It was as hard at home as it was in the desert, in some respects it was harder.

As dusk approached, we decided to go back to The Badger Pit. As we drove up the highway, we passed hundreds of Abrams M1A1 tanks and numerous Multiple Launch Rocket Systems (MLRS) encamped at the Jabail turn-off. "I think we're really going to reek some havoc," said Woody, surveying the equipment. We passed a truck with a homemade sign painted on the back: "Grand Opening Coming Soon: Kuwait City." The January 15th deadline was now only three weeks away.

NOTE:
The satellite dish we acquired from Ghost Town turned out to be ineffective without an expensive decoder. I turned it over to LTCmdr Hopkins who operated Armed Forces Radio in Saudi Arabia. His sergeant was so happy to get the dish that he allowed me to make an on-air dedication. I dedicated one of my favorites, "Another One Bites the Dust," to Saddam Hussein.

Getting Wired in Saudi Arabia

With the introduction of the new PX refrigerator and microwave at The Badger Pit, the demand on our 15KW generator often exceeded recommended levels. Sometimes the draw was so great, that the generator simply shut itself down. This was a major problem as our communications equipment required a constant power source. Rationing seemed to be the only solution to keep continuous power to our communications. The electricians proposed that TVs, VCRs and radios only be played during certain scheduled hours and that lights be kept off except in work areas. Power tools and machines would have scheduled use only. The hue and cry that arose over the proposal resulted in SFC Dave Schneider coming to see me with a request for a new generator.

The next morning SGT Crum, Stoney and I were on the road before six a.m. Like most good soldiers of today, I was armed with memorandums, requisitions and written justifications. We made the hour drive to the Port of Jabail and began the search for a new generator. We checked supply houses, warehouses, Navy stocks and port holding areas. No generator could be found. Undaunted, we drove the additional hour to Dammam and began the search anew. We checked at every supply and holding area in Khobar, Dammam and Dhahran. Just after dinner, we finally found what seemed to be the only 30KW generator in the Middle East. We didn't actually find the generator itself, but we did find paperwork indicating that a 30KW generator was being held by the 321st MMC. After fighting a maze of red tape, I landed in the office of a LTC Ward. LTC Ward sympathized with our predicament. Using his rank, he led me through the labyrinth of paperwork necessary for secure a material release order allocating the generator to our unit. It was now after ten at night. I borrowed a radio from the 321st and called up to The Badger Pit requesting that a large truck be sent down to pick up our new-found power source. SGT Crum, Stoney and I then went to the storage yard and waited. At ten minutes after one in the morning, SPC Joel Schloesser pulled up in a 5-ton truck. SPC Randy Stratman was with him in the cab. Both of these truck drivers were body builders and fairly big-boned besides. It took the pair less than fifteen minutes to load the generator and get us back on the road north. I was satisfied that I had completed a successful day's work. On the way back to The Badger Pit, I slept.

At seven o'clock the next morning two of our electricians, SPC Dave Mathison (Sparky) and SPC Frank Arado (Franco), awakened me. Sparky heaped on the praise for acquiring the generator. He told me how great it was and how it was a prize he truly loved and, for Sparky, I am sure it bordered on love. Things electrical were his lifeblood and of any person in the unit, Sparky appreciated results. The praise kept coming, however. As much as I wanted to sit there and wallow in the lime light, I smelled a rat. "Alright, Sparky!" I said finally, "What is it you want." Sparky and Franco explained that the generator would only satisfy the company's thirst for power if we had the wire to hook it up. The wire we currently used was getting too hot and could not handle the additional power. We needed something with a thicker gauge. Another emergency mission was about to start.

I sent for SGT Crum and within the hour we were beginning the two hour drive to Dhahran. As a necessary exercise in futility, I checked the regular supply channels. I was told that if we ordered the wire immediately, they emphasized immediately, we could possibly hope to receive it by spring! Obviously, this was an unacceptable answer. I recalled that our group headquarters, located at The Expo, was at this time wiring air conditioning into their dining tent. While their access to wire was unlimited, mine was now nonexistent. I was never really fond of our group headquarters. They had developed a practice of taking care of themselves before taking care of the troops under them--the troops in the field. They were always long on inane orders, however. They once sent out a memo directing that all soldiers should have polished boots at all times and that saluting officers should not be set aside simply because we were in a field environment. It didn't take a computer genius to see the absurdity of the orders. Saluting an officer in the field is called "sniper check" because any snipers in the area would immediately kill the saluted person--it was a bad practice. And, while polishing boots is a good idea, so as to keep the leather supple, keeping them polished throughout the day was not possible in the ravaging desert sand. CPT Berg snorted when he read the orders. He handed them to First Sergeant Kaderavek who simply let them get lost in the shuffle.

While our group headquarters placed emphasis on saluting and boot polish, my emphasis was on completing the mission to which I was assigned. Right now my mission was acquiring wire. SGT Crum and I drove to the group's fancy dining facility. We found the wire, just as I had recalled, spooled and ready for use. I went in to see the supply officer while SGT Crum went to radio back to the unit for a truck. The supply officer gave me the same song about ordering the wire immediately so that we would have it by spring. With a little coaxing, however, I got him to say that we could have any wire that they might have. He believed, of course, that they had none. He would soon be right.

I walked out the door and met SGT Crum. The message had been sent and a truck was on its way. We went back to Bill's Bar and Grill, drank

NA beer and waited. By noon, SPC Joel Schloesser and SPC Randy Stratman, who had picked up the generator the night before, arrived with a 5-ton truck. It was now as simple as throwing the wire in the bed of the truck and our power problems would be solved. We grabbed the wire and counted, "1,2,3. . . lift!" The wire didn't budge. We tugged, we pryed, we leveraged. Nothing could get the wire from the ground to the truck. I saw a forklift operator unloading crates at the far end of the parking lot. I recognized him from supply. With all the brass of a full bird colonel, I marched over to the operator and directed him to load the wire. Dutifully, the wire was loaded and within minutes we were on the road. The only thing that now lay between us and The Badger Pit was a shawarma stop and a phone call home!

WAR!

President Bush had warned Iraq to withdraw from Kuwaiti territory by the January 15th deadline or face military action. Hussein stayed, perhaps thinking that American resolve had been fatally injured by the Vietnam Conflict. He thought wrong. At 0244 January 17th, America went to work. Almost thirty different American aircraft had some part in the Desert Storm that swirled into Iraq. By war's end, more than 100,000 combat sorties had been flown in support of the war. And an estimated 150,000 Iraqi troops perished as a result of the relentless bombing brought about by Hussein's intransigence.

C-47 Chinook loading ammunition at The Badger Pit.

SCANNING HORIZON: Brig. Patrick Cordingley, commander of the British 7th Armored Brigade, scans the horizon in the Saudi Arabian desert early Wednesday morning from the turret of his Challenger tank.

arab news

SAUDI ARABIA'S FIRST ENGLISH LANGUAGE DAILY

Published simultaneously from Riyadh, Jeddah, Dhahran and Cairo

VOL. XVI NO. 52, FRIDAY, JANUARY 18, 1991 -- RAJAB 3, 1411 A.H. 12 PAGES, 2 RIYALS

MISSILES: Sparrow missiles are carried out to U.S. Marine F-18 fighters on Wednesday. The Sparrow, when fired, can travel at speeds in excess of 2,660 miles per hour and cover a distance of 30 nautical miles.

ce List : ☆ Bahrain 100 Fils ☆ Egypt 1 P ☆ India 12R ☆ Japan 250Yen ☆ Jordan 250 Fils ☆ Kuwait 100 Fils ☆ Lebanon 300L ☆ Republic of Yemen: Sanaa R 3.00 - Aden 100 Fils ☆ Oman 200P ☆ Pakistan 12R ☆ Philippines 25P ☆ Qatar 2QR ☆ Singapore 3 $ ☆ Sudan 2P ☆ Syria 6L ☆ Thailand 40BHT ☆ U.A.E. 2D ☆ U.K. 50P

The day of 1,000 air sorties

AIR STRIKE: A Royal Saudi Air Force pilot atop his fighting machine minutes before he was airborne to strike targets deep in Iraq on Thursday. The graphic at left by the Associated Press depicts the first aerial assault on Iraq. -- (*Arab News* photo by Giovanni Pasquale)

Iraqi Air Force crippled
Scud missile attacks foiled
• Turkey OKs use of force

CENTRAL SAUDI ARABIA, Jan. 17 (Agencies) -- Saudi warjets, British Tornado fighter-bombers and Kuwaiti jets joined the U.S. air attack on Iraq today pummeling strategic targets with more than 1,000 sorties in hours. French Jaguars joined the second wave a few hours later.

They hammered air bases, missile sites, chemical weapons plants, command centers -- even targets in the heart of Baghdad.

Armed with U.N. authorization to go into action against Iraq, allied forces began the assault before dawn. Pilots spoke of little resistance. There were no ground battle today.

U.S. Defense Secretary Dick Cheney and Gen. Colin Powell, Chairman of the Joint Chiefs of Staff, expressed satisfaction with the initial results of Operation Desert Storm -- but both stressed that there could be other casualties in a protracted campaign to drive Iraq from Kuwait.

Military sources reported the first U.S. death in the operation came when a Navy FA-18 fighter attack jet was shot down.

Other military sources said indications were the plane was downed by a surface-to-air missile, but exact details were still under study.

The plane was said to be from the aircraft carrier USS Saratoga, stationed in the Red Sea.

"There have been casualties and there are likely to be more," Cheney told reporters at a mid-morning briefing. Cheney also noted that a British pilot appeared to have been lost during the combat operation.

Powell said the bombing "damaged the command and control capability of the Iraqi government," as well as airfields, Scud missile installations and other targets.

At the White House, President George Bush declared the wave of air strikes against Iraqi forces "successful as much as possible," and met with congressional leaders as the nation awoke to Gulf war today.

However at his news conference, Cheney cautioned against premature claims of victory over Iraq.

In London, British Prime Minister John Major confirmed that a British Tornado fighter-bomber had been shot down.

In Paris, Defense Minister Jean Pierre-Chevenement said four French Jaguar planes had been hit during a raid over Kuwait's Al-Jaber region, but all pilots returned safely.

The French Defense Ministry later reported that all four planes had been repaired and were ready for action. One pilot suffered slight facial cuts.

Kuwait announced the loss of a fighter jet in the day's military operations, the Kuwait news agency KUNA reported today.

The agency quoted Sheikh Sabah Al-Ahmad, the defense minister as saying the plane was lost "while performing its mission within the homeland," that is flying against emplacements of Iraqi forces occupying

Continued on back page (The day)

Bush ready to stop if Saddam pulls out

WASHINGTON, Jan. 17 (Agencies) -- U.S. President George Bush said today allied forces will not halt their war against Iraq unless Baghdad leader Saddam Hussein fully complied with United Nations demands.

"We are not going to stop until he (Saddam) fully complies with the (U.N.) resolutions," Bush told reporters on the periphery of a White House cabinet meeting. Responding to reporters questions whether Saddam should surrender, Bush said, "he can call it anything he wants ... but we are going to prevail." U.N. motions include a demand for an unconditional pullout of Kuwait.

Earlier the White House today called on Iraqi President Saddam Hussein to withdraw from Kuwait, after U.S. military officials said the first day of continuous air strikes devastated Iraq's military machine. "If at any point he wants to change course here, all he has to do is surrender and comply with all the U.N. resolutions," Presidential press secretary Marlin Fitzwater told a news briefing. By "surrender" Fitzwater said he did not mean Saddam had to surrender Iraq or give up his leadership, merely leave Kuwait as the United Nations demands.

King Fahd hails allied forces

RIYADH, Jan. 17 (SPA) -- Custodian of the Two Holy Mosques King Fahd stated today that the military operation, which began early this morning to liberate Kuwait represented "the sword and sound of truth." He extended greetings to all forces arrayed against the Iraqi regime and wished them victory. Addressing an extraordinary session of the Coucil of Ministers at Yamamah Palace here today, King Fahd said: "It was inevitable to make things in order and implement the United Nations resolutions that demand the liberation of Kuwait, and we invoke God that He might register victory for His army."

King Fahd deplored Iraqi President Saddam Hussein's intransigence toward peace calls. "I myself advised President Saddam on many occasions to return to God's order, avoid bloodshed and protect the lives of innocent people, but he refused, displayed arrogance... and rejected the call of truth, justice and peace."

He noted the efforts of world leaders to spare the Gulf region a devastating war, but, the king added, Saddam intended to trigger it (war) by refusing to pull out of Kuwait.

King Fahd briefed the ministers about the outcome of his contacts during the last two days to convince Saddam to come to his senses.

Prince Sultan, second deputy premier and defense and aviation minister, also briefed the council on today's military operation against Iraq.

Meanwhile, Interior Minister Prince Naif urged citizens and residents to abide by the Kingdom's rules and regulations and not to involve in any activities aimed at jeopardizing the country's security and stability. "We would like to see security and stability prevail and things going smoothly all over the Kingdom," he added. Violaters will be punished under Shariah law, he said.

Saudi Arabian pilots do the nation proud

By Aldo Svaldi
Gulf Bureau

SOMEWHERE IN EASTERN SAUDI ARABIA, Jan. 17 -- Jet fighters of the Royal Saudi Air Force streaked down the runway at a base here, lifting into the air with a deafening roar as blue fire poured out of their tails.

Within 10 minutes eight planes were counted heading for targets deep within Iraq. In cavernous hangars nearby other planes were loaded with bombs, preparing to head out in what is becoming one of the most massive aerial attacks in history.

Saudis have been flying together with Kuwaiti, U.S., U.K. and French pilots in Operation Desert Storm to liberate Kuwait. The Saudis have been piloting U.S. made F-15s and British made Tornado jets.

Years of training have paid off for the Saudi pilots, who are doing well in their first acid test. As of this report, no Saudi planes have gone down. One American journalist commented that the young men have flied and fought with a precision that should be a source of national pride.

Tornado pilots like Lt. Muhammad Al-Ahmary and Lt. Muhammad Hussein have been attacking Iraqi air bases, trying to prevent planes from using the runways.

Their calling cards are huge craters, which prevent the Iraqi Air Force from taking off. Lt. Hussein said he destroyed the runways at the Lo Gibbah and Sheiahair base.

Although flying at a great speed, Lt. Hussein said he could see smoke and fire rising up from the runways he destroyed.

Saudi pilots interviewed expressed surprise at the lack of resistance on the past of Iraqi pilots, most of whom have chosen to run rather than fight. They said they had yet to confront an Iraqi pilot.

Saudi planes flying over Iraqi territory were met with cannon fire and SAM missiles, which they dodged. The greatest difficulty one pilot said, was picking out the targets.

Precision on the part of pilots is especially important, as allied air forces are trying to avoid civilian casualties as they attack military sites, Col. Abdullah ibn Khalid ibn Turki said.

Among the sites hit within Baghdad during the first 12 hours, according to CNN, are the Ministry of Defense, the communications center, the Tigris refinery, Baath Party headquarters, and Air Force headquarters.

Pilots returning from bombing runs said resistance was much lighter than expected, according to pool reports. Anti-aircraft artillery provided some difficulty, but Iraqi planes were a rare site.

Continued on back page (Saudi)

Ground attack imminent

By Wahib M. Ghorab
Arab News Staff

SOMEWHERE IN EASTERN SAUDI ARABIA Jan. 17 -- Massive air and missile attacks by the multinational forces blasted and destroyed the Iraqi air defenses. The attacks appear to have been very strong as there was no reported resistance in any of the fronts.

The air strikes have obtained desired results, depriving the Iraqi Army of an air cover.

The forces here are well-equipped with night vision glasses as well as other gadgets vital for night combat. Helicopters capable of causing heavy damage to the Iraqi forces in the region are all set for action.

The coming few hours will see heavy ground fighting. We saw the units moving toward Kuwaiti border.The 101st Airborne Division has special duties and will probably be among the first to enter Kuwait. The unit is here well trained for night fighting.

Reporters in the news pool learned about the impending air strike at 9 p.m. when a state of alert was announced yesterday.

The morale of soldiers is very high. One

Continued on back page (Ground)

Iraqis in for hammer blows after air raids

By Ed Blanche

News Analysis

NICOSIA, Cyprus, Jan. 17 (AP) -- Allied air strikes against strategic targets in Iraq are likely to continue for another day or so to knock out mobile missile batteries and command centers before starting to soften up Iraqi troops in Kuwait, analysts say.

"They'll keep the pressure on over the next 24 hours. Then, if the Iraqi ground forces have shown no sign of giving up, they'll go after them," said veteran Mideast military analyst Hans-Heino Kopietz.

"If I was an Iraqi ground commander, I'd be throwing in the towel," the London-based Kopietz said in a telephone interview.

"The Iraqis have no idea what it's like to be constantly hammered from the air. It's not something they had to contend with in the war with Iran."

The key objective on the second day of the Gulf conflict appears to be to destroy Saddam Hussein's air force before any allied ground offensive is launched to liberate the emirate he conquered Aug. 2.

Another is to eliminate the threat from mobile surface-to-surface missile units capable of hitting, possibly with chemical warheads, the multinational troops and armor waiting to move against the estimated 540,000 Iraqis in the Kuwait theater.

Allied officials have not yet issued any detailed assessment of the damage done by the hundreds of U.S., British, French, Saudi Arabia and Kuwaiti jets which bombed Iraq today or the Cruise missiles launched from the U.S . battleships Missouri and Wisconsin.

Reports from Cairo quoted informed Saudi sources as saying that an estimated 85 percent of Iraq's surface-to-surface missiles were destroyed today. But Iraq has given no indication of the damage.

Analysts believe that most of Saddam's estimated 36 fixed surface-to-surface missile launchers were destroyed along with 100-150 of the Iraqi Air Force's 700 aircraft.

That would still leave the Iraqis with considerable firepower.

Continued on back page (Iraqis)

Kuwaiti rulers return in 10 days

By Saeed Haider
Gulf Bureau

DHAHRAN, Jan. 17 -- The Kuwaiti government hopes to enter Kuwait after 10 days and it has completed all the arrangements in this regard, according to Dr. Abdul Rahman Al-Awadi, minister of state for cabinet affairs.

Addressing a news conference here at the Joint Information Bureau, the minister said the government had put on stand by a medical team and other necessary facilities somewhere in the Eastern Province. He said the air raids by the allied forces have not affected the center of the country. Some damage was reported

Continued on back page (Kuwaiti)

International community reacts swiftly, hopes for an early end to hostilities

HAMBURG, Jan. 17 (Agencies) -- The international community reacted swiftly today to the news of the outbreak of war in the Gulf with most government leaders expressing their "deep sorrow" and hopes that hostilities would end soon.

Perhaps the most favorable reaction to war's outbreak was on world financial markets, which surged on the apparent initial success of the overnight air strike against Iraq. Oil prices, which had been expected to rise, dropped instead.

Around the world, allies of the United States not participating in the attack -- including Japan and South Korea -- strongly supported the action. Most Middle East governments reacted cautiously.

In the Soviet Union, which approved the U.N. Security Council resolution allowing force against Iraq after Jan. 15, armed forces were put on high alert along the nation's border with Iraq early today.

President Mikhail Gorbachev gave a national address to "express our deep sorrow that military confrontation could not be averted." He reassured Western allies that "the Soviet Union will go on cooperating with other countries and the United Nations." But he urged U.S. President Georgh Bush to make one last attempt to contact Saddam Hussein.

China, another U.N. Security Council member, which abstained from the vote, urged restraint among the warring nations. "We still call for peace and hope that the flames of war will not spread or expand," said Foreign Ministry spokesman Li Zhaoxing.

But on the streets of Beijing, some people enthusiastically backed the attack as they snatched up newspapers and huddled around radios for war news.

Among Washington's strongest allies, German Chancellor Helmut Kohl said he learned of the attack with "deep dismay."

Other world leaders echoed the sentiments of a crestfallen Javier Perez de Cuellar, the U.N. secretary-general whose 11th hour peace initiative failed. He wondered how war had erupted "after all my efforts, after the efforts of so may countries, so many different personalities."

The European Community expressed its "deep regret" that war had become necessary. "Only a withdrawal of Iraqi forces from Kuwait would prevent new victims and new destruction," said a statement issued by Luxembourg on behalf of the 12-nation trading bloc.

For some, it was a day of jubilation. Kuwaiti exiles poured out of their homes in the Gulf state of Bahrain and filled mosques to pray for victory. Women had tears streaming down their faces.

Other Mideast countries reacted with caution. Jordan closed its international airport, and Iran expressed "deep regret" at the outbreak of war. But in Syria, the newspaper of the ruling Baath Party blamed Iraq's Saddam Hussein for the war, saying, "No one can shed a tear for this regime."

Egypt, with more than 36,000 troops engaged with the multinational anti-Iraq forces, also endorsed the attack.

Hungary, Czechoslovakia and Romania all voiced support for the effort to free Kuwait. There were also protests from some grass-roots opponents of the invasion around the world.

Japan's morning rush hour was in full swing when news of the attack hit the streets. Crowds converged on newsstands loaded with extra editions blaring huge three-inch headlines.

In Islamabad, Pakistan Prime Minister Nawaz Sharif said today the Gulf war carried "the potential of a global catastrophe", the official radio reported.

Indian Prime Minister Chandra Shekhar today expressed anguish at the outbreak of war in the Gulf, saying Asia will bear the consequences of the fighting. "India and other Asian countries will bear the brunt of the war, in a great way," he said in New Delhi. Shekhar called for an emergency meeting of the chief ministers of all Indian states later in the day to study the impact of the war.

In Manila, President Corazon Aquino expressed firm support today of the actions of the U.S.-led multinational forces against Iraq.

"The Philippines reiterates its adherence to and support for the United Nations resolutions on this crisis," Mrs. Aquino said in a nationally televised address hours after the coalition forces bombed targets in Iraq.

"The Philippine government supports without reservation the action of the coalition forces led by the United States," she said.

"We note with approval and relief the stress made by President Bush that the goal of the military action is not the conquest of Iraq, but the liberation of Kuwait to the end that both states may soon once more stand in peace among the family of nations," she said.

A South Korean government spokesman expressed backing for the initial stage of the move to punish Saddam Hussain.

"We wholeheartedly support the decision of the United States-led multinational force to punish Iraq for its continuing uncivilized acts," Information Minister Choi Chang-Yoon said.

Australian Prime Minister Bob Hawke went on national television to announce he had authorized three Australian ships in the Gulf -- HMAS Sydney, HMAS Brisbane and HMAS Success -- to take part in the United Nations-approved offensive to oust Iraq from Kuwait.

"We, all of us, wish for peace, but we cannot have peace just by wishing for it, or by talking about it," Hawke said. "We have to work for it and sometimes, tragically, we have to fight for it."

In Bangkok, Thai Prime Minister

Continued on back page (International)

F-117A Stealth Fighter designed to be virtually undetectable to enemy radar.

On the morning of January 17th, the company clerk woke Stoney, Hackman and me around two a.m.. A message had been received raising our danger status to Threat Level Delta--attack imminent! The entire company donned its gas warfare equipment, including mask, and waited. This would be the first of many Scud alerts that would send us scurrying for protective gear. The continuous roar of jets could be heard overhead although no trace of them could be seen in the still dim twilight. We waited all night. We listened to the BBC and Armed Forces Radio for any shred of news. None came. Up to now, it had seemed almost like a military exercise. Over the next five days, scores of Iraqi Scuds would hit Israel and Saudi Arabia.[14] The exercise was over. Reports of damage were always discounted by official sources but for those injured, killed or displaced, the attack was all too real.

Children in Hafar Al Batin pose in front of their home that was destroyed by a Scud missile.

---

[14] The Scud B similar to its sister missile the Al Hussein, was 37 feet long, 3 feet around and carried a payload of 2,172 pounds.

Within a few days of the commencement of the air war, operations at The Badger Pit nearly ceased. No ground elements were expending ammunition and all transportation assets were being directed toward moving combat material north. Therefore, we continued to wait. Hours seemed to move like days and days like weeks. Most nights we would get Scud alerts. We would go to MOPP Level 4 and wait for the Scud to impact somewhere in Saudi Arabia.[15] Sometimes the attacks seemed more dangerous than at other times. Occasionally, when the threat seemed most severe, we would be ordered to take bromide tablets. The bromide purportedly worked as a catalyst for the atropine injectors that we carried everywhere we went.[16] A few of us,

---

[15] MOPP Level 4 meant that a gas attack had occurred or was imminent and that all gear should be worn. MOPP suits (mission-oriented protection posture) consisted of rubber, camouflaged coat and pants lined with a charcoal insulator, rubber boots and gloves, a protective mask and a rubber helmet cover.

[16] Chemical weapons fall into four categories. Nerve Agents: Iraq had Tabun gas and the very lethal Sarin gas; Blood Agents: Iraq had several including hydrogen cyanide; Blister Agents: Iraq made extensive use of mustard gas in its 8-year war with Iran; Lung Agents: Iraq could easily have made numerous lung agents, such as chlorine gas, by mixing chemicals.

who spent significant amounts of time in Iraqi primary target areas like Dhahran, even received anthrax vaccinations.[17]   The days were relatively quiet.   The jets still screamed overhead, sometimes so low that they only appeared for moments before they were lost over the next dune.   Most days I had business in Dhahran.   I would usually awake around four-thirty or five and, with SGT Crum, would begin the morning with the barren two hour drive south.   Sometimes the work was with our battalion, sometimes with ARCENT and most times it was at various places down the hundred mile corridor through Jabail and Khobar.   As though I weren't busy enough, I was assigned the additional duty as battalion liaison officer.   This basically meant that I became responsible for all the unit's administrative problems.   In addition, I had become almost manic about my supply mission.   Once given a request, I usually didn't

---

[17] Anthrax, commonly referred to as Wool-Sorter's Disease, has plagued man since antiquity.   Anthrax is a spore-forming germ that comes in four forms.   The form adapted for military use is pulmonary anthrax. Pulmonary anthrax is caused by inhalation of the anthrax spore.   It usually results in death 18 to 20 hours after ingestion.

quit until the requisition had been filled. I would beg from private companies, borrow from other units or trade at the ports. I thrived on the challenge of accomplishing the impossible. During my various excursions, I had the opportunity to meet many different people in a variety of occupations and departments. Therefore, whenever one of our soldiers was having trouble, I usually knew someone who could help. A few people expected miracles that couldn't be delivered, but most were appreciative for what little was done. Overall, we were an outstanding success.

On one occasion, Stoney and I had spent the entire day shuttling between our battalion and ARCENT, tracking down ammunition shipping directives and supply requisitions. We finally got what we needed around nine p.m., so we decided to stop by the American Corner and have a shawarma before completing the two hour drive north. The stores at the American Corner were either closed or vacant as much of the civilian population now remained at home after sunset. The nightly Scud attacks closed all but Safeway and Kentucky Fried Chicken at the shopping center. Their windows were covered with tape to prevent shattering. Stoney and I ate our shawarmas and talked with reporter Tim Collie of The Tampa Tribune. Reporters seemed oblivious to Scud attacks, enemy fire and even terrorist attacks. Near ten o'clock we decided to begin our trek home. We inspected the Blazer, like we did every time it was left unattended, then crawled inside to begin our trip. We were about to pass Souks Supermarket when we noticed that there was no one waiting to use the telephones. We pulled over and called home. It was quiet now and I figured it would be a good time to call Joel De Spain at WISC-TV to let him know that everyone was well. Just as the anchorwoman Beth Zurbuchen answered the phone, a shrill horn sounded in the distance. Khobar looked like a ghost town. It was another Scud attack! I pulled out my gas mask and placed it on the phone. I wanted to complete the call to allay the concerns of families with soldiers in the Gulf. Quickly, I gave her a list of names and dedications that I had collected from soldiers. I told her all was well but I couldn't hide the wailing siren that foretold of another attack. I hung up the phone with a promise to call back within a few days time. No sooner had I placed the receiver back onto the telephone, when a screeching Patriot missile sliced through the night sky and careened into an incoming Scud! The continuous clicking from Stoney's camera sounded like gunfire as the burning fireball fell harmlessly in the distance. Two hours later, when we reached The Badger Pit, the Scuds were still coming.[18]

The American Patriot missile played a pivotal role in destroying many of the Scuds before they impacted. Unfortunately, it was not a fool-proof system. Twice, Patriot-intercepted Scuds hit targets much more important than they probably would have. In one instance, a downed Scud spewed debris over an ammunition storage area in Dhahran with no major damage but with the potential to have been the single worst allied

---

[18] On that night, January 20th, 1991, U.S. Patriot missiles intercepted at least nine Scuds aimed at Saudi Arabia. Unfortunately, Stoney's pictures of the Scuds were too dark to be developed using the slow speed film in his camera.

event of the war.[19]   In another instance, an intercepted Scud produced the heaviest American casualties of the entire conflict.   Two days before the Iraqi surrender, a military holding site directly behind Souks Supermarket was destroyed by an Iraqi missile.   Twenty-eight American soldiers were killed and nearly a hundred wounded.   It was only by luck that Stoney and I weren't in Dhahran that night as we usually were.   Ironically, we were near the Saudi/Kuwaiti border where we felt in significantly greater danger.   Little did we know....

---

[19]The Scud fallout covered the area in and around Theater Storage Area 1 (TSA 1) in Dhahran. The amount of ammunition stored at the sight measured in the hundreds of thousands of explosive pounds. Had the Scud destroyed the site, both civilian and military casualties would have been high.

Skibbie

It was a welcomed relief when, on one January morning, we received orders to take-on additional operations at Corps Storage Area 11 (Skibbie). Skibbie was located about fifty miles northwest of The Badger Pit near a small town called Nuayriyah. Our mission would be to move the stored ammunition out of Skibbie and to the frontline troops or to other storage areas. When we were assigned the additional task of operating Skibbie, it was no more than a pile of sand. Much needed to be done to bring it up to parity with The Badger Pit. Hackman was in charge of ammunition at Skibbie and together we planned another American oasis. We opened a branch PX and put in hot showers. Then we went foraging. The Whackers, who since our Christmas expedition were now trained scavengers, were members of the 2nd Magazine Platoon that was part of the Skibbie detachment. They began by digging a three foot pit in their tent and building a sunken living room! SPC Mike Zientek, SGT Charles (Charlie) Brown and SGT Paul Frank led their squads through the surrounding dunes, scavenging any useful items. The terrain around Skibbie was more hilly than that at The Badger Pit. Buried within the valleys, the scavengers found some very promising circumstances. The area immediately around our encampment had recently been a staging area for combat support units. They apparently evacuated the site in some haste as was evident by the mass of supplies they left littered throughout the dunes and scattered across the desert floor. Construction materials, sand bags, lumber and even military equipment like poison gas alarms had been abandoned. At one location I found two fully operational refrigerator vans completely filled with fresh fruit imported from Lebanon. Within a hundred yards of the vans, I discovered over a quarter million bottles of pure drinking water. Interspersed with the water were 15,000 cartons of multi-flavored irradiated milk: chocolate, vanilla, strawberry and even banana! I went back to Skibbie for help. SGT Paul Frank, SPC Comers, SPC Dornacher, SPC Kidd and SPC Schloesser all volunteered for service. With my driver, SGT Jeff Crum, we were seven. SGT Frank's crew loaded a forklift onto a forty-foot trailer and followed us back toward the abandoned treasure. As we drew near the stacks of food and materials, we discovered that we were not the only scavengers of the desert. Marines from Combat Service Support Detachment 10 were hand loading a five ton truck as fast and furiously as they could move. They stared in amazement as we downloaded the forklift and began to move supplies onto our forty foot trailer.

SGT Paul Frank, SPC Bob Gruenwald, SGT Troy Bennett and SPC Mike Zientek show a little leg.

We long ago discovered from the troops at Jabail that "cooperation" was a Marine's middle name. They never turned a deaf ear on calls for help and we knew it. We tried to reciprocate in some small way by using our forklift to load their truck with water, milk and wood. Our goodwill was repaid when the leathernecks told us about a location some twenty-five miles north that had cases of chocolate M&Ms and Campbell's soup. They showed us their haul: twenty-four boxes of M&Ms and fifty cases of soup. Like flies to road kill, we moved out across the desert to salvage the abandoned food. The milk and water would wait.

SGT Crum and SGT Frank had jumped in the front seat of a pickup truck. The Skibbie volunteers had piled-in the back. The forty-foot trailer followed closely behind. As the pickup jolted and tossed over the uncharted road, I could hear howls of laughter from the now shaken passengers. The louder they howled, the faster they went! I went back to Skibbie to get an operator to retrieve the forklift that we had left sitting near the water.

Drawing near the location designated by the Marines, an unexpected sentry appeared on the road. The guard, an American born and bred, realized that if he gave away all the soup and M&Ms, he would no longer have to stand duty. Without the aid of forklifts or cranes, the Skibbie crew packed and loaded the entire forty-foot trailer with Campbell's soup and chocolate M&Ms. It was dark when they completed their work. One hundred and twenty-five thousand cans of soup and 12,500 packs of M&Ms were on their way to The Badger Pit! MREs were now a thing of the past![20]

Our additional duty assignment at Corps Storage Area 11 (CSA 11)--"Skibbie."

---

[20] At the conclusion of the war, the people of Kuwait City lacked many of the basic food stuffs. The 826th Ordnance Company delivered MREs, M&Ms and Campbell's soup to those liberated from Hussein's occupation. The work of the Skibbie crew was appreciated more than they ever knew.

Skibbie was about an hour's driving distance from The Badger Pit, so SGT Crum and I planned to stop by Nuayriyah on the way back for a shawarma. It was now nearly eleven p.m. The small local souq was in full operation owing to the Saudi's unique business hours. We bought a shawarma and a Pepsi and talked about the day's lucrative haul. The conversation had evolved into a discussion about Army food when two GIs pulled up. They were from the 101st Airborne Division that had set up an encampment thirty miles to the north of Nuayriyah. The biggest of the two, SSG Bennett, ordered two shawarmas and they sat down to join us. Sgt Crum and I proudly related the story about the flavored milk, the water, the soup and the M&Ms. I went to the truck and retrieved a case of candy for them. "Have you tasted the 'Top Shelf' stuff?" asked Bennett. We hadn't even heard of it. The Army was apparently running out of MREs and had made a major purchase of a retail food called "Top Shelf." I vaguely remembered seeing it at a grocery store back in The States. It sounded great: Salisbury steak, noodles and sirloin tips, macaroni and cheese and even lasagna! "Anybody this far north can get it," said Bennett. "Its available from the S&S unit on the corner of MSR Mercedes and MSR Dodge." We were only five miles away! We finished our shawarmas, wished the guys "good luck" and went to seek the "new MREs."

When we pulled into the compound just after midnight, it was evident that this was the right place. Flood lights poured over the trucks loading the new meals. There were also Styrofoam cups, called "Lunch Buckets," full of rigatoni, ravioli and beef stew, macaroni, caccitori and chili. Combined with the "Top Shelf," we were about to significantly improve our chow facilities. We were sixth in line for service. When the sergeant finally got to us, he explained that we would need a form 1366, a form 2602 and a form 3308 before we could draw rations. Once we had these, we could draw as much as we needed. The notion that you could talk your way around military red tape was a fabrication of American TV. We would get what we needed only when the sergeant had the forms. We departed for The Badger Pit.

When we arrived, another Scud alert was beginning. It was now after two a.m. I sent SGT Crum to get a few hours sleep before leaving again the next morning. The mess crew was already beginning to prepare the morning meal. I found the mess sergeant and told him the location and the forms necessary to get the new food. Within an hour he was on the road. Dinner the following day was great. We had soup, lasagna, strawberry milk (or NA beer) and M&Ms! We sat outside in the darkness and listened to the air war on Armed Forces Radio. The Air Force was flying about 2,000 sorties per day over Iraq. There was pinpoint bombing and carpet bombing. Either way, the bombing was continuous.

As I sat there with Stoney and Hackman, I heard someone yelling my name. "Hey LT! LT!" I turned to see JD dressed only in white Arab head gear and brown underwear. "Did you hear that the Soviets sent ten ships to the Gulf yesterday?" His hands waved as he talked.
"That's great!" I said. "We need all the help we can get."

"There's only one problem," JD was beginning to crack a smile. "The Mexicans don't know what to do with them!" He laughed and walked off toward the outhouse.

"He's a good troop." I said to no one in particular. "They're all good troops," Hackman said, again to no one in particular.

LT and Hackman

SPC Steve Steffen and SPC Greg Mauel

SPC Mike Masse and SGT Steve Deignan

SGT Dan Grover and SGT Ed Comstock

SPC Mike Zientek and SPC Travis Youngs

SPC Norman Edgington and SPC Caryn Elliott

SSG Jeff Reed and SPC Scott Lins

1SG Lon Kaderavek and SSG Lindy Weinman-Bong

SPC Mike Est and SPC Fred Schumacher

SFC Jim Esser, SFC Joe Franklin and SSG Lloyd Dunn.

126

AL KHAFJI ATTACKED!

The term "supply" in Saudi Arabia was really a misnomer. The supply system was nonexistent for items such as wood, hammers and nails. This was due in part to the extensive logistical problems encountered by operating 10,000 miles from home, and in part to an ineffectively run local purchasing program. To compound these problems we were 110 miles north of Dhahran and I did not have a vehicle! Initially, when everyone was in need, vehicles were more readily available to me. By the end of January, however, critical needs had been filled and vehicles were like good Army meals: everyone's heard of them but nobody's seen one. It was especially hard to coax sections to release vehicles for seek and salvage missions. These were the most unpredictable but often the most lucrative type of mission. Armed with non-alcoholic beer for trading, I would simply drive out into the desert until I spotted allied troops. I would then trade NA beer for other Army supplies, based upon our unit's needs. Eventually, care packages arrived from home containing real alcohol which opened almost every door in the military supply system. Outsiders were often amazed by The Badger Pit. Among other things, our facilities included four color television sets with VCRs, a theater-sized popcorn popper, a Ping-pong table, volleyball and basketball courts and even an outdoor weight room!

SPC Melissa Peterson, SPC Kevin Peterson and SPC Troy Sater watch on as the troops play volleyball (horseshoe pit in foreground and basketball court in background).

SPC Clint Oppermann, SGT Jeff Crum and SPC Corey Statz in Khafji.

A major problem had been dogging our vehicle the further we proceeded north: the fuel tank was drying up! At first, the problem did not seem dire because we were confident that we could get diesel commercially in the city. I had long ago discovered on a mission to Riyadh that commercial fuel was very inexpensive--18 cents/gallon in most instances and only $3.60 to fill our twenty gallon tank.

As we entered Khafji, however, we were struck by the haunting feeling that something was terribly wrong. There was no one in sight. This town of thirty thousand people had been evacuated leaving us no place to get diesel and

SFC Jim Esser, SFC Joe Franklin and SSG Lloyd Dunn.

AL KHAFJI ATTACKED!

The term "supply" in Saudi Arabia was really a misnomer. The supply system was nonexistent for items such as wood, hammers and nails. This was due in part to the extensive logistical problems encountered by operating 10,000 miles from home, and in part to an ineffectively run local purchasing program. To compound these problems we were 110 miles north of Dhahran and I did not have a vehicle! Initially, when everyone was in need, vehicles were more readily available to me. By the end of January, however, critical needs had been filled and vehicles were like good Army meals: everyone's heard of them but nobody's seen one. It was especially hard to coax sections to release vehicles for seek and salvage missions. These were the most unpredictable but often the most lucrative type of mission. Armed with non-alcoholic beer for trading, I would simply drive out into the desert until I spotted allied troops. I would then trade NA beer for other Army supplies, based upon our unit's needs. Eventually, care packages arrived from home containing real alcohol which opened

SPC Clint Oppermann, SGT Jeff Crum and SPC Corey Statz in Khafji.

A major problem had been dogging our vehicle the further we proceeded north: the fuel tank was drying up! At first, the problem did not seem dire because we were confident that we could get diesel commercially in the city. I had long ago discovered on a mission to Riyadh that commercial fuel was very inexpensive--18 cents/gallon in most instances and only $3.60 to fill our twenty gallon tank.

As we entered Khafji, however, we were struck by the haunting feeling that something was terribly wrong. There was no one in sight. This town of thirty thousand people had been evacuated leaving us no place to get diesel and leaving the Marine detachment, we found ourselves on a hard-surfaced road headed straight north. The first sign we passed was written in Arabic and was undecipherable. Soon, however, an English sign notified us that we were at Rass Meshaab Port--only a short fifty miles or so from Al Khafji and the Kuwaiti border! Khafji had been in the news about a week prior to our expedition because it had come under attack from an Iraqi artillery barrage. The allure was too great a temptation and we unanimously decided to seek and salvage on the Kuwaiti border in Khafji!

As we had done on our crapper caper, we negotiated the road blocks and check points with relative ease. Even before entering Khafji we were assured of a successful mission. A small Bedouin tent had apparently fallen out of a truck along side the road and it looked and smelled to be the real McCoy! It would be a good break tent in our work area. We threw it in the back of the truck next to Corey and Clint and continued north.

On January 27, 1991 very little ammunition was being shipped from The Badger Pit or Skibbie. Even though work was light, it took nearly an hour of searching before I acquired a vehicle for a seek and salvage mission. My driver was again SGT Crum. Our brothers-in-arms on this expedition were Specialist Corey Statz and Specialist Clint Oppermann. The vehicle I had acquired was a pickup. After it was dispatched, Corey and Clint hopped in the bed of the truck and SGT Crum and I got up front. We loaded with NA beer and moved out into the desert to procure yet unknown supplies. By the very nature of the mission we had no set destination. It so happened that we headed north, bounding across the desert to see what lay over the next sand dune. Like a Rat Patrol unit we bounced over the drifts and flew over the dunes until we spotted elements of a Marine combat service support unit. We stopped and talked with the supply sergeant, negotiating a simple transaction. In exchange for some non-alcoholic beer, we acquired plywood flooring for use in our Skibbie tents. We made arrangements to have the flooring delivered the next day and once again proceeded north. Within forty-five minutes of almost every door in the military supply system. Outsiders were often amazed by The Badger Pit. Among other things, our facilities included four color television sets with VCRs, a theater-sized popcorn popper, a Ping-pong table, volleyball and basketball courts and even an outdoor weight room!

SPC Melissa Peterson, SPC Kevin Peterson and SPC Troy Sater watch on as the troops play volleyball (horseshoe pit in foreground and basketball court in background).

our pickup was already reading "E." The lack of even military personnel punctuated the air of abandonment about the town. Our situation was growing desperate. We knew there were no troops to the south from where we had just come so our only alternative was to move north on the road, hopeful that Coalition Forces must stop us somewhere over the few kilometers that now lay between us and the Iraqi positions. Our confidence in this eventuality began to fade as the complete absence of anything military grew more and more obvious. Crawling up the coast at a snail's pace to conserve what little fuel we did have, we saw the bellowing smoke from a civilian oil storage tank that had been hit by Iraqi artillery and the windows from so many buildings blown through by explosive concussions. Across the border we could hear the purr from the American "Vulcan" machine guns and the blasts from the F-16's cluster bombs as the air war pounded the enemy fortifications. Although we had front row seats to the war, we felt uneasy by our inability to flee if it became necessary.

The empty streets of Al Khafji hours before the Iraqi invasion.

As the sun began to set on the horizon, we discussed whether we should set up camp for the night or proceed a little further north. The consensus was that we should proceed for two of the five kilometers that now separated us from the Iraqis and then set up a bivouac sight. As we crept up the coast toward the Iraqi front, we joked about spending the war in a POW camp. We would call it Stalag 13 after the television show Hogan's Heroes. Our jokes masked the trepidation we were feeling as we drew nearer the bomb blasts. Finally, with less than 3000 meters to the border, we saw a Saudi Arabian checkpoint consisting of four soldiers and two vehicles. It was not much, but our relief was immense. Sgt. Crum pulled the pickup along side the checkpoint. The soldiers had locked and loaded their machine guns and trained them on our vehicle. Very slowly we removed our military identification cards and handed them to one of the soldiers. After a careful inspection, a smile raced across his face. I believe he was as nervous as we, and as delighted to see another friendly force. Through sign language and pointing excitedly at our fuel gauge we conveyed our problem. I was able to understand that they too had very little fuel. Beyond the fuel in their trucks, they had one five gallon jerry jug that was less than 2/3's full. We tried to convey the import of our situation but to no avail. They had no desire to be caught without fuel within a stones throw of the front line. I could hardly blame them. We were ready to pitch our tents and wait for a patrol team when the Saudis spotted two boxes of MREs in the back of the truck. With the same excited tones we had used to describe the diesel, they now pointed to the MREs and to their mouths. A barter was in the works. Heated discussions about the value of the diesel in relation to the MREs took place in both English and Arabic with neither side understanding the other. Finally, with the emergence of an English-Arabic dictionary, we agreed that they would give us the little fuel they had in exchange for the MREs, provided that we returned the next morning with a full five gallon can. We were in no position to refuse. We accepted and poured the diesel into the truck, ensuring that not a drop was wasted.

With a new lease on life we now moved south toward Rass Meshaab Port. The sun fell below the horizon as we left Al Khafji and the buildings flashed their silhouettes against the exploding American bombs on the receding border. We drove in silence over the vacant, dusty road toward Skibbie, stopping only long enough to fuel the truck at Rass Meshaab.

Back at Skibbie we planned our next day's departure. Sergeant Crum and I would leave at first light and return to Khafji with fuel and more MREs. "Not a word to anyone," I ordered the crew. They all agreed, thankful to have made it back to camp, but more thankful to have had the adventure. I ate an MRE for supper and passed out on my sleeping bag until four a.m. when Sergeant Crum shook me awake. We loaded the vehicle with fuel and food and moved out toward Khafji.

The Al Khafji Beach Hotel before its Iraqi occupation.

As we approached the first road block we saw immediately that a chemical alert had been ordered. The road guard was in his complete chemical suit: a rubber, camouflaged coat and pants lined with a charcoal insulator, rubber boots and gloves with a protective mask and helmet.

"Get out and get in your gear!" he yelled. "The Iraqis have just attacked Saudi Arabia!" We jumped from the vehicle and began to don our gear.

"They've attacked just north of here!" His voice was full of excitement. "They've taken over the town of Khafji!" We froze at the mention the the town.

"Al Khafji?" I asked.

"Yes sir!" he yelled through his mask, "They've occupied it!" I looked at the full fuel can in the back of the truck and the cases of MREs.

"I hope they made it out." I whispered to SGT Crum,.

"God!" he said, "I hope so too."

"At least we were fortunate enough not to have any Americans in the area." I said.

"I don't know." said the guard, " A tractor-trailer from the 11th Transportation Company passed through here not more than an hour ago."

"You better radio that in," I advised.

"I guess I'd better." he said. "There were two drivers--a male and a female."

"They were probably going to meet someone coming in from the desert," I said.

"Let's hope so, sir." the guard responded.

137

Little could we have imagined that America's first female POW of the war was now in Iraqi hands. Specialist Melissa Rathban-Nealy and Specialist David Lockett had inadvertently turned north on the same tapline road we had traversed. The mistake placed them in the path of the invading Iraqis.

We turned back toward Skibbie. Advancing clouds of dust grew on the horizon as Marines and helicopters moved north. Only the luck of having met the Saudi guards the previous day had kept us from spending the night in Khafji. Unfortunately, the transportation Specialists weren't so lucky. The ground war had started and the town of Al Khafji, on the Saudi/Kuwaiti border, was now the eye of the storm.[21]

---

[21]Within two days U.S. Marines and Saudi army units would completely rout the Iraqi army from Khafji.

KKMC Revisited. . . and Again

By the middle of February, Coalition ground forces were poised and ready to strike. The wettest desert winter in over twenty years continued to plague our operations as well as those of the combat units. Still, no attack orders arrived and everyone waited. Air sorties had exceeded 80,000 by February 18th and estimates of Iraqi war dead were rumored to be approaching 100,000. To date, less than 100 American soldiers had been killed in action, although the ground war was expected to dramatically increase this number. While the waiting war dragged on, I continued to work. As always, my plans were hindered by the availability of transportation. Finally, I resolved to concentrate my efforts on acquiring a truck exclusively for my own use. I let it be known at battalion and other places I frequented that any information concerning the availability of vehicles would be greatly appreciated. CPT Ginni Bradford contacted me a few days later. Seventh Corps had apparently turned in all their Blazers in exchange for off-road vehicles. Although their trucks were in dubious condition, I had confidence that our maintenance people could make them fully operational, if I could acquire any of them.

My first foray on what turned out to be a 2000 mile expedition began at The Badger Pit and took me back to the 321st MMC located in Dammam. I had been told to seek out a CPT Ashworth at the 321st but when I arrived, I found that he had been redeployed to KKMC. The VIIth Corps Blazers, on the other hand, were located at Log Bases Alpha, Bravo and Charlie throughout northern Saudi Arabia. If we drove from Dammam to just north of Hafar Al Batin, we would pass through Log Bases Alpha and Charlie. Log Base Bravo was located just outside KKMC where Hackman and I had already visited. I checked with LTC Ward at the 321st and was assured that if I successfully located CPT Ashworth, I would be authorized a vehicle. LTC Ward had helped me once before when I fought through the red tape to acquire a 30KW generator, so my confidence began to grow. From the 321st, I drove over to our battalion to complete the paperwork. On a whim, I wrote up the paperwork authorizing our unit an additional three vehicles instead of just one. This meant that if I were successful, I would need at least three drivers to get the vehicles back--if we received any at all!

Accompanying me on this expedition were SFC Adam Mekschun, SFC Joe Franklin and Stoney. Adam was another Vietnam veteran although, unlike Hackman and Stoney, he had served his tour as an infantryman. Perhaps because of his Vietnam experience, Adam exuded an intense persona that bordered on being overbearing. At his very best, he was pointedly direct. Joe, on the other hand, was amiable and friendly. He was over 55 years old and a grandpa. Perhaps that is why we got along so well; I really liked Joe.

We left at seven o'clock the next morning moving north up MSR Dodge toward Log Base Alpha, Hafar Al Batin and finally KKMC. The road was in its usual state of disrepair although elements from the US Army engineers were making some improvements. We passed a sign erected by the 864th Eng. Bn. that read: "Your highway dollars at work--Drive Safely." The sign more appropriately should have read, "drive defensively." The road (MSR Dodge) was perhaps 24 feet wide with no shoulder and no passing lane. The hodgepodge of large military vehicles interfered with traffic flow so that speeds varied from 25 mph to 65 mph, depending upon oncoming traffic. Interspersed with the military vehicles were excitedly impatient civilians who apparently bore little fear of death. Most of the civilian trucks were loaded way beyond capacity and were so old or dilapidated that their mere presence constituted a hazard. It was easy to understand why the sides of this desert road were covered with discarded wrecks.

One of many wrecked vehicles that littered MSR Dodge.

Dodging and weaving our way over the road, we finally reached the 778th Maintenance Company at Log Base Alpha where some of the Blazers were being held. As we pulled into the right side of the gate, over a hundred Blazers were pulling out of the left side. I was beginning to suspect an Army conspiracy existed intent on subverting my vehicle request. The gate guard told us that all VIIth Corps vehicles were being transferred to the 165th Supply Company at KKMC. We turned around and got back on the road toward Hafar Al Batin and KKMC, in hot pursuit of the VIIth Corps Blazers. Twenty miles before Hafar Al Batin, we stopped at a roadside gas station for an MRE lunch. After battling the sand flies for half an hour, we moved out again.

SFC Joe Franklin, SFC Adam Mekschun and Stoney having an MRE lunch at a local gas station

At Hafar Al Batin, I noticed a significant change in the people. The air war had been going tremendously well for the Coalition Forces and the sense of relief felt by these local inhabitants was apparent. Even when a Scud missile destroyed several houses in the city, they still felt secure behind the Coalition front. As we drove through the town, everyone smiled and waved the victory sign. The change was heartwarming. From Hafar Al Batin we turned south on MSR Sultan and proceeded toward KKMC.

Anytime we were on the road, Stoney and I played a form of trivial pursuit to while away the hours. For example, I would ask him who *Time* magazine named "Man of the Year" in 1938 or what is the only state over which no foreign flag has ever flown. He, in turn, would usually stump me with questions like, who pitched the only perfect game in World Series history?[22]

---

[22] In 1938 *Time* named Adolf Hitler as "Man of the Year." Idaho is the only state over which no foreign flag has ever flown. New York Yankee pitcher Don Larsen pitched a perfect game against the Brooklyn Dodgers on October 8, 1956.

The majesty of KKMC had not diminished since my last trip, although it may have been tainted by the thousands of troops and tents that filled every available space. Our first order of business was to locate CPT Ashworth of the 321st and attempt to procure a materials release order. We found the 321st and the 165th Supply Company, who physically controlled the vehicles, next to each other at Log Base Bravo on the outskirts of KKMC. We stopped at the 321st and were told by Lt. Lewis that no MROs would be issued without approval from Col. Ellis or LTC Bandini at the 22d Support Command (SUPCOM). The conspiracy to stop my vehicle request seemed to be growing. We drove the short distance from Log Base Bravo to central KKMC. This military city had exploded in population. Prior to the war it contained somewhere around 5,000 soldiers. Now its population exceeded 25,000 soldiers and was growing everyday! I found Col. Ellis without too much difficulty and presented my request for three vehicles.

I was once told that: "If you're not a sergeant or a general, you're still in training." This included colonels too. Every full bird colonel I ever met was all brass tacks and business. They told the straight scoop from the start. Only when they were promoted to general would "maybe" become a part of their vocabulary. Col. Ellis was no exception. He was still in training to learn the mastery of politics required to get his first star. He told me that I could submit my requisition with a memorandum of justification and I would "go on the list." I got the impression from him that the list was held in a circular file cabinet. Undeterred, however, I spent the next hour composing and typing a memo. When it was finished I again presented it to Col. Ellis. This time he fobbed me off to LTC Victor J. Bandini. Where Ellis was a down-to-business colonel, Bandini was a gentle, well-tempered lieutenant colonel. His prospects for promotion to full bird were dismal in light of his good natured personality, but if he ever made it to colonel, he'd go all the way to general. I knew this when he gave me the dreaded "maybe" and told me to return in two days--as though I lived just down the street. I walked to the parking lot where Adam, Joe and Stoney had been patiently waiting for nearly two hours now. I didn't have the guts to tell them we had driven all day for a "maybe," so I told them I simply had to return in two days and our vehicles would be available.

By now the darkness enveloped everything. We decided to head back to The Badger Pit with a short detour through Hafar Al Batin. We were no more than a thousand yards into the darkness when our headlights fell upon an unwound bale of concertina wire strung across the road. Adam swerved sharply but the Blazer picked up the wire, wrapping it around the rear axle and ripping the pinion seal. Adam slammed the brakes and we jumped out just in time to see the last drops of oil seeping through the U-joint. Figuring that some oil must still be in the axle, we immediately drove to the nearest camp. Coincidentally, this camp belonged to the 165th Supply Company who controlled the VIIth Corps Blazers that we so desperately needed. Their motorpool sergeant SFC Hanneman, assessed our damage. We weren't driving anywhere in our Blazer. Hanneman explained the problem to their NCO on duty, SSG Wright. The sergeant began to work through the NCO Corps trying to release one of the coveted Blazers that they held. SFC Hanneman helped find a safe location for our truck until it could be repaired. Any unsecured, broken vehicle in Saudi Arabia was little more that a mobile junk yard. Parts and supplies were so hard to come by that anything resembling a broken vehicle was picked apart within hours. With a little coaxing from SSG Wright, the 321st finally agreed to release a Blazer to us "for one week." The conspiracy to subvert my vehicle requisition was beginning to crumble. Within an hour, we were on our way. We drove all night long, arriving at The Badger Pit just after four a.m.

We woke the next morning around seven and prepared for our return visit to KKMC. This time, besides Stoney and Joe, I took SSG Ed Comstock who was a very competent mechanic. Adam spent the morning diligently locating a pinion seal. I knew that parts were nearly impossible to get through military channels, and could give him little guidance. Adam needed no guidance. Using the maxim: "Anything to accomplish the mission," he drove for forty-five minutes to the city of Jabail and purchased a pinion seal from a GM dealer with his own money. With the new pinion seal in hand, we left The Badger Pit just after noon for our return trip to KKMC.

When we arrived at the 165th Supply Company in early evening, we found our vehicle just as we had left it. I looked for SFC Hanneman but he couldn't be found. SSG Mike Olson, whose job it was to inspect all the Blazers being turned in by VIIth Corps, volunteered to help. This National Guard unit from Savannah, GA consisted of the finest gentleman the south had to offer. With little difficulty, SSG Comstock dropped the drive line and tore away the wrapped concertina wire. The muted expletives that emerged from under the truck told us that the damage exceeded the pinion seal. The entire rear end had been destroyed! We would need a whole new axle if this vehicle was to ever operate again. SSG Olson was right there to help. He suggested that we talk to his company commander who could authorize us taking a rear-end off a damaged vehicle. His C.O. readily agreed to give us a new axle from a damaged vehicle provided we exchanged the broken axle so that all the trucks could at least be towed. We happily agreed. It was now nearly seven in the evening and our light had been reduced from the desert sun to three hand held flashlights. SSG Olson excused himself for a few minutes. When he returned he was driving a huge tow truck with attached flood lights. For the next three hours, Stoney, Joe and I, under the direction of SSG Comstock, hooked, unhooked, torqued, pulled and hammered at the vehicle until we were once again operational. We were dirty, tired and hungry but appreciative of the 165th Supply Company.

SSG Mike Olson of the 165th Supply Company works with SFC Joe Franklin.

SSG Olson had heard of a place nicknamed "Hotel California," somewhere between Log Base Bravo and central KKMC. Hotel California provided transient quarters for soldiers passing through the area. With our two vehicles, we sought out a place to wash, eat and sleep. In the darkness of the desert night, we passed Hotel California and ended up stopping at the 21st Replacement Detachment. After we explained our predicament, they agreed to let us sleep in one of their troop quarters. The NCO in charge told us to find a cot in the first tent. There were three tents, easily the largest I had ever seen. They were about sixty feet wide and four hundred feet long and housed approximately five hundred soldiers each on this night. Entering the first tent we found ourselves in the midst of an infantry battalion preparing to move north. We sought out four vacant cots, which were the last four in the building, and bedded down for the night. Two minutes after we lay down the shrill howl from the air raid siren filled the encampment. The infantry soldiers moved as they had been trained and within seconds had their chemical protective masks on. Someone turned off the lights. We had been through these raids so many times that we were becoming complacent. Somewhat out of place in the tent, now lit by flashlights, Joe, Comstock and I put on our protective masks. Stoney, on the other hand, immediately crawled into his sleeping bag and zipped it over his head. He had apparently forgotten his protective mask at The Badger Pit. He knew that he would be the unfortunate center of attention if he were spotted, so he was attempting to hide. The battalion Command Sergeant Major began at the far end of the tent checking each individual. The check consisted of no more than a flashlight beam to ensure that everyone was masked. The inspection was inconsequential to everyone but Stoney who was still buried in his sleeping bag. As the CSM drew closer it was apparent that Stoney was about to be embarrassed beyond imagination, not to mention that this was a real Scud alert and the mask might really save his life! The CSM stopped momentarily to speak with a soldier who was having difficulty clearing his mask. He proceeded with his inspection. He drew within two cots of me, then flashed his light on Comstock. Stoney was next. Just as the light flashed by me, the lights came back on and the all clear was sounded. Stoney popped his head out from under his sleeping bag. He was gasping for air like he had been held under water. I laughed at his predicament but couldn't help thinking about what might have happened had a chemical Scud impacted in our area. I recalled a graphic verse by Wilfred Owen from the poison-filled trenches of the First World War:

Gas! Gas! Quick, boys!--An ecstasy of fumbling,
Fitting the clumsy helmets just in time;
But someone still was yelling out and stumbling,
And flounde'ring like a man in fire or lime. . .
Dim, through the misty panes and thick green light,
In all my dreams, before my helpless sight,
He plunges at me, guttering, choking, drowning.

If in some smothering dreams you too could pace
Behind the wagon that we flung him in,
And watch the white eyes writhing in his face,
His hanging face, like a devil's sick of sin;
If you could hear, at every jolt, the blood
Come gargling from the froth-corrupted lungs,
Obscene as cancer, bitter as the cud
Of vile, incurable sores on innocent tongues,--
My friend, you would not tell with such high zest
To children ardent for some desperate glory,
The old Lie: *Dulce et decorum est*
Pro patria mori.[23]

---

[23]"Lovely and honorable it is to die for one's country"

The Command Sergeant Major appeared at five the next morning for wake up. No one seemed too excited about getting out of bed but we four visitors. The infantry wouldn't get out of bed until it was required at second call. I didn't blame them. After a breakfast consisting of a banana and irradiated milk, we went looking for our sister unit from Wisconsin, the 395th Ordnance Company. We found them operating the ammo dump at Log Base Bravo, in conjunction with the 351st Ordnance Company from West Virginia.[24] Stoney, who had been in our unit seventeen years, knew many of the 395th's soldiers. I met the recently assigned company commander CPT Dick and shook hands with the executive officer CPT Bertrum, whom I had met sometime before in the United States. After a short visit, I figured it was time to visit LTC Bandini to check on the status of my vehicle request. Whereas my first visit to the 22d SUPCOM took more than two hours, this visit lasted not more than five minutes. LTC Bandini informed me that all Blazers were going to civil

---

[24] The 664th Ord. Co., who had initially run the operations when Hackett and I visited, had been transferred north.

154

affairs units in preparation for the administration of Free Kuwait. I asked about vehicles that were deadlined--an Army euphemism for inoperative. He told me that I could have as many deadlined trucks as I needed. With our unit's great mechanics, it would be no problem to get at least one vehicle operational if we could get enough parts. I asked for three vehicles and my request was approved on the spot. Stoney, Joe, SSG Comstock and I, then went to the 321st to have an MRO issued and then to the 165th Supply Company to actually pick up the Blazers. Olson was working again and I told him we were successful in getting three deadlined vehicles. As the inspector for the vehicles, he knew which ones were good and which ones were junk. He picked two Blazers deadlined because they were missing brake hoses and one deadlined because of a faulty switch. Comstock reinspected the vehicles and agreed that they could all be made operational with only minimal work. To us, this was the equivalent of getting three fully operational vehicles. I went to take care of the paperwork and Comstock went to work on the Blazers. SSG Olson let him scavenge parts off other deadlined vehicles. By the time I returned thirty minutes later, the work was complete. We now had three additional Blazers. The Army supply system amazed me. I couldn't get an operational vehicle because they were needed elsewhere, but I could get vehicles that took a good mechanic a half an hour to fix. We now had five total vehicles: our original Blazer with the repaired rear end, the Blazer we had on "one week loan," and the three we just acquired. Comstock hooked-up a tow bar to one of the vehicles and we each drove another back to The Badger Pit.[25]

Our newly acquired vehicles at KKMC before our drive back to The Badger Pit.

---

[25] We successfully received several extensions on the Blazer we had for the "one week loan." The unit eventually returned it, five months later.

KUWAIT CITY LIBERATED!

On February 24th at four a.m. The Badger Pit received another alert. The Coalition Forces were beginning the ground war against Iraq! From our location, we could see everything moving north: tanks, helicopters, APCs and troops. Throughout the day I read intel reports that described fierce but successful fighting by American troops. At nearly every location the Iraqis were being overrun. The Iraqi front shrunk deeper and deeper into Kuwait. By the third day, the Iraqi front disappeared altogether. Coalition Forces had so far suffered very light casualties, while successfully capturing nearly 50,000 prisoners. More fighting was expected, however, when the forces reached Iraq's elite Republican Guard that Hussein had placed in northern Kuwait. During the entire ground war there was little activity in The Badger Pit. I spent most hours reading reports from the front that were so full of excitement that I could scarcely contain myself. Finally, I covered my schedule for the next few days and plotted a course that would take me to the front line. Chief Stone also got excited when I told him of my plan and together we entered a conspiracy. Our excursion to the front was propelled by curiosity and adventure. During Stoney's tour in Vietnam, he had come under heavy shelling but he had never been able to meet the enemy face to face. He felt that this was his chance. We began early the next morning. With stores of fuel, food, ammunition and water, we figured to move northwest up MSR Dodge to Hafar Al Batin. We would then turn north on MSR Sultan and proceed up the interior road to Kuwait City. MSR Dodge seemed surprisingly vacant that morning and we made good time on the road. It was now day five of the ground war. As we moved north, the news came over Armed Forces Radio that the Coalition advance had been halted, although fighting continued in and around Kuwait City. The war looked to be over for the Iraqis. POWs were pouring in to all locations and no sustained resistance was reported on any front. Coalition Forces could have occupied all of Iraq by the next day if the President so ordered. I admired his restraint. The United Nations had only authorized the removal of enemy forces from Kuwait, not the invasion of Iraq. America's foreign policy would be enhanced by the

President's decision to stop where his international mandate ordered.

As we reached Hafar Al Batin, a Saudi MP sped by with lights flashing and siren blaring. Close behind, he escorted seven civilian Land Cruisers belonging to an American Army civil affairs unit. I punched the accelerator and fell in behind them. For the fifty-five miles from Hafar Al Batin to the Kuwaiti border we followed the police escort, passing troops and tanks at speeds approaching 100 mph. When we reached the border, the police slowed to stop although there were no guards or checkpoints. I shot through the demarcation too excited and too full of adrenalin to pause now. What had been a small, two lane road in Saudi Arabia, branched out into a four-lane, divided highway in Kuwait. The devastation from the war was immediately visible. Systematic precision bombing had carved huge craters in the road at precisely 100 meter intervals. These craters were approximately ten feet wide and eight feet deep, making the road impassable. Pock marks from the 20mm machine gun carried by the "Tank Killer" A-10 aircraft were also occasionally interspersed between the craters. Scattered about the road were the unlucky recipients of the Coalition air power: tanks, armored personnel carriers (APCs), trucks, cars and even motorcycles. Iraqi helmets, gas masks, uniforms and weapons lay everywhere. We spotted an unexploded cluster bomb and stopped to investigate. On one side of the green bomb an American Air Force soldier had written some jocular remarks: "Do you get the feeling that this just isn't going to be your day?" Beside the bomb and littered throughout the battlefield, were small white strips of paper. I picked one up and read the inscription that was written in both English and Arabic:

CEASE RESISTANCE-BE SAFE
TO SEEK REFUGE SAFELY, THE BEARER MUST
STRICTLY ADHERE TO THE FOLLOWING
PROCEDURES:

1. REMOVE THE MAGAZINE FROM YOUR WEAPON.
2. SLING YOUR WEAPON OVER YOUR LEFT
SHOULDER, MUZZLE DOWN.
3. HAVE BOTH ARMS RAISED ABOVE YOUR HEAD.
4. APPROACH THE MULTI-NATIONAL FORCES'
POSITIONS SLOWLY, WITH THE LEAD SOLDIER
HOLDING THIS DOCUMENT ABOVE HIS HEAD.
5. IF YOU DO THIS, YOU WILL NOT DIE.

We scanned the battlefield. In addition to the litter of personal combat gear, we could see gaping craters from the heavy pounding these soldiers had taken. Further down the road we came to the infamous "pits of oil" that were to be set ablaze in an attempt to stop the Coalition advance. The onslaught had been so fast, however, that the pits still remained full and unburned. Beyond the pits lay Iraq's most dangerous weapon: mine fields. I had seen reports indicating that some Iraqi mines contained poisonous gas and had even heard a report that four American soldiers had died from a gas mine. As the American combat engineers plowed through these lethal defenses, they had simply stacked the mines alongside the road. To the east and west of the breach, lay thousands more mines, still buried. The Iraqi's next line of defense consisted of twenty-foot wide stretches of tanglefoot: a type of barbed wire strung in a crisscrossed fashion about six inches above the ground. It was impossible to crawl under and very difficult to navigate on foot while under fire. The Iraqis had prepared for a war like the one they had recently completed with Iran. They were completely unprepared for the

modern, computerized, mechanized force that
was thrown against them.

اوقف القتال الآن حافظ على حياتك

من اللجأ، يجب من .... بالخطوات التالية:
للبحث بالسلام
١. اسحب مخزن الذخيرة من سلاحك.
سلاحك على كتفك الايسر مع توجيه الماسورة الى الاسفل.
٢. احمل
٢. ارفع يديك فوق راسك.
من مواقع القوات المتعددة الجنسيات ببطء ولي فرد في
٤. اقترب
المقدمة يرفع هذه الوثيقة فوق رأسه.
٥. اذا عملت هذا تنجو من الموت.

CEASE RESISTANCE - BE SAFE

To seek refuge safely, the bearer must
strictly adhere to the following procedures:

1. Remove the magazine from your
weapon.

2. Sling your weapon over your left
shoulder, muzzle down.

3. Have both arms raised above your head.

4. Approach the Multi - National Forces'
positions slowly, with the lead soldier holding
this document above his head.

5. If you do this, you will not die.

Leaflets dropped from an American cluster bomb.

162

The famous pits of oil the Iraqi Army was to ignite when the Coalition push began. The advance was so quick and the Iraqi surrender so rapid, that the pits were never burned.

Concertina wire and tanglefoot that the Iraqis stretched for hundreds of miles along the border. It was of very little hindrance to the American combat engineers who breached the barricade with no problems.

Beyond the tanglefoot, was stacked concertina wire extending along the border as far as the eye could see. Our combat engineers had cut through these defenses like an afternoon exercise but always under the threat of death if they didn't perform their jobs properly. The success of the advance showed that they performed with perfection. Once behind Hussein's "Maginot Line" we saw more destruction: more tanks, more APCs, more trucks, more cars and now the occasional body of an Iraqi that had not yet been picked up by the Saudi litter details that combed the countryside. The bodies were covered with sand flies voraciously sucking precious, sweet fluids. There was surprisingly little smell. If not picked up within a few days, the decomposing corpses would bloat until, on one hot afternoon, they would explode.

To our left, we saw dug-in fighting positions. We turned off the road and moved in toward the bunkers. The reports we'd heard of heavily dug-in forces was no more than propaganda to forestall any better preparation. The Iraqi front line looked like a scene from WWI. Trenches, approximately 24" deep, extended for miles, with fighting and sleeping positions placed every forty feet or so. The fighting positions were atrocious attempts at fortification. They consisted of a hole six by four feet by 18" deep-- six inches higher than the trenches to keep water and rodents out. The hole was covered with corrugated tin and lightly sprinkled with sand. Any explosion would have shredded the tin, sending bits and pieces in every direction. The Iraqis had virtually covered themselves with shrapnel! One thing was clear: the Iraqis had vacated in haste, either surrendering or running northward. The trenches were full of light armaments: grenades, rocket-propelled grenades (RPGs), bullets, mortars, AK-47 assault rifles and even an occasional flame thrower.

Stoney in an Iraqi trench inspecting the ammunition.

Craters along the main road leading from Hafar Al Batin
to Kuwait City.

A Soviet made T-54 tank that fell victim to the air war.

We left the trenches and moved north toward Kuwait City. The closer we drew toward the city, the greater the destruction. To the credit of the allies, however, much of Kuwait's infrastructure had been left intact. Bridges, overpasses, sewer and electrical lines had escaped destruction unlike Iraq where the annihilation was near complete. Only Kuwaiti communications facilities were completely destroyed by allied attacks. A large bomb had decimated a central Kuwaiti telephone station and the skeletal remains of satellite dishes could be found everywhere. As we neared the city the sky grew so black with smoke that it became impossible to determine the time without referring to a watch. The smoke was bellowing from oil fires that encircled the Kuwaiti capital. In a senseless attack on future revenues, Iraq had blown-up hundreds of oil wells. It was an ecological disaster. Occasionally, light winds would open pockets of sunshine around the city. Eventually, the winds became so heavy that the smoke passed south and west of the capital leaving the town temporarily free from the hazardous fog. On the outskirts of the city we crossed an overpass upon which sat a large anti-aircraft gun and the makeshift quarters of the soldier who had recently manned it. The gun was cocked and ready to fire. Numerous shell casing, remnants of attacks on Coalition planes, were scattered about. We continued along the highway awed by the burned-out vehicles and equipment that were littered about. People began to line our route, a few at first and then hundreds. They cheered us as victors, but more, they cheered their escape from repression. Among these people waving homemade Kuwaiti flags and cheering, I noticed the conspicuous absence of males between the ages of 16 and 50. The crowds consisted of children, women and old men. We waved continuously at these joyous people and slowed to shake hands with the children who ran alongside the truck. One small child pointed to his mouth and seemed to be asking for food. We had packed twenty-four MREs and saw no harm in parting with a few of them. The response was immediate. We were swarmed by hundreds of starving woman and children whose wrenching eyes and crying voices begged for food. We handed out all of the MREs we had brought but were still buried in the mass of hungry people that enveloped our truck. Children climbed all over the vehicle yelling their agonizing pleas for food. Their starving faces were all we could see. Just as our options began to close in around us, a Saudi Arabian security vehicle pulled along side. With halted Arabic shouts, the soldiers cleared our path. Thankfully and remorsefully we drove into Kuwait City. The hungry, silent faces of the women and children followed us, their jubilation momentarily interrupted by the reality of their terrible predicament. In every child, I saw the faces of my own daughters. I nearly cried as we left them starving along the roadside. I was determined that I would return with more food.

A jubilant crowd celebrates as we enter Kuwait City hours behind the Iraqi withdrawal.

An Iraqi anti-aircraft gun on the outskirts of Kuwait City was cocked and loaded to fire.

American aircraft targeted command and control centers like this Kuwaiti telephone switching center. All that remained of this ten story building was the reinforced stairwell.

The Meridian Hotel in downtown Kuwait City was looted and destroyed by the Iraqi troops.

LT searching a destroyed Iraqi tank in Kuwait City during the final hours of the war.

It is often by happenstance that people find themselves at world events. Such was our case as we turned onto the Coastal Road in downtown Kuwait City. A spontaneous celebration consisting of people and vehicles stretched for miles along the sea coast, past the British and American embassies and through the central district where hotels, shops and restaurants had been gutted and ransacked by the Iraqis. With horns blaring and flags waving, the people chanted, "George Bush!" "George Bush!" "George Bush!" Hundreds of people shook our hands and in various forms of English said, "Thank you very much--very much!" Some could not hold back their tears. They cried on the sidewalk while waving their country's flag. The air was electric with the excitement of freedom and hope for the future. One woman stepped forward, her right eye severely disfigured from some unspeakable injury. She handed me a Kuwaiti flag roughly sewn from red, white and green cloth. She was not the only victim of the Iraqi barbarism. Numerous people had open sores or burns. One woman waving at us had stripes branded onto her hands and arms as though she had been held against a hot grill.

A spontaneous parade to celebrate the allied liberation
of Kuwait City. The horrors that had been inflicted
against the children sickened me.

We eventually turned off the celebration route
and moved northward. The torture the Iraqis
had inflicted sickened me. But as we moved
north, it became apparent that the United States
Air Force had exacted revenge. The Iraqis, who
had looted, pillaged and terrorized the city only a
few days before, had attempted to flee with their

booty by whatever transportation was available: stolen vehicles, police cars, trucks, ambulances and even bicycles. As the escaping soldiers fled toward the city of Basrah in southern Iraq, attack planes closed off the road by destroying the lead vehicles. They then cut off the retreat back to Kuwait City by blasting the trailing vehicles. Between these two points the Air Force collected the toll for Hussein's incursion into Kuwait. By nightfall a ten mile long exodus had turned into a collection of bodies and equipment that were burned, shot and charred beyond recognition. The smell of burning rubber combined with the hot, sooty air from the raging oil fires punctuated the finality of this battle. We stopped the truck and I got out and stood on the Blazer's roof. To the north, the road snaked around a hill. To the south, the body of the snake coiled around Kuwait City. As far as I could see in both directions were the charred remains of the Iraqi Army. Some vehicles had been turned over, others blown apart. Some had been completely engulfed in flames destroying whatever or whomever was within. A few had been immobilized simply by their lack of an escape route, their occupants killed. Only those very few who left their stolen goods and ran from the area with white surrender flags were spared their lives. Stoney and I continued north. Our exclamations of incredulous awe were repeated a hundred times over until we reached the head of this snaking exodus. We turned back southward. This time we drove silently through death valley and into the thick pall that encompassed southern Kuwait.

An Iraqi soldier who had been fleeing from a ravaged Kuwait City with his booty when the American Air Force caught-up to him

This had been an emotional day for me: starving children, torture, destruction, death and in some sense, hope. We passed a convoy of military trucks filled with food. For the people of Kuwait the nightmare was now over, help was on the way.[26]

LT handing out MREs and candy. Many children that were left homeless or orphaned clustered along the roads in search of food.

---

[26] When we returned to The Badger Pit with our story, the unit decided to take much of our extra food to Kuwait City. Several times over the next week Stoney and I took MREs and Campbell's soup to the people of Kuwait City.

Searching for more food.

The destroyed vehicles that the Iraqi Army had stolen to carry their booty back across the border. No one survived the American onslaught without surrender.

Miles and miles of destroyed vehicles littered the road.

Epilogue

The conclusion of the war brought celebrations throughout the world.   At the 826th, however, the celebrations had to wait.   While Stoney and I continued ferrying food to Kuwait City, Hackman was ordered to take over operations dealing with captured enemy ammunition.   His Blazer was now almost always filled with Iraqi mines, grenades, RPGs and explosives.   Eventually, Stoney and I were ordered to join Hackman.   We three amigos once again found ourselves together.

Near Khobar Towers, which was the largest American military holding site in Saudi Arabia, we cleaned and crated Iraqi Scud and Frog missiles.   With an entire country of barren wasteland to choose from, it struck me as ludicrous to place these enemy explosives so close to inhabited areas.   Fortunately, we worked without incident.   Finally, more than three weeks after the Iraqi surrender, Hackman, Stoney and I celebrated the victory.   With a few of the Whackers, we planned an expedition across the Saudi border to Bahrain for some well deserved R&R.   Although it is a devoutly Muslim country, Bahrain does not forbid the sale of alcohol.

The island country of Bahrain lies about ten miles off the coast of Khobar, Saudi Arabia. A beautiful, new bridge stretches out from Khobar to connect the two countries. The bridge also acts as a border post. On March 17th, 1991, with all of us packed into Hackman's Blazer, we drove out of Khobar and onto the Bahrain Bridge. We didn't have any border passes, but the guards didn't seem to mind as long as we were American soldiers.

Our first stop was the U.S. Navy's recreation center, where we could buy beer and alcohol at American prices. I was the designated driver, so I drank only Pepsi. Everyone else drank Jack Daniel's with beer chasers. At ten o'clock sharp, the Navy recreation center closed its doors. I poured the Whackers back into the Blazer and took them to downtown Manamah, Bahrain's capital city. Unlike Saudi Arabia, Bahrain retained very little of its old structure. With only 231 square miles in the entire country, land was significantly more precious than on the mainland. We drove through the downtown area. High rise office buildings with bank or industry logos displayed across their tops dominated most city blocks. The seemingly thousand year old souq had not yet been disturbed by the modernization, however. After our short tour, we stopped at the Holiday Inn and went into the nightclub. The bar was decorated with an orange-red carpet and dark orange wall coverings. The chairs and the entire bar table were built from a dark wood that toned down the reds and oranges. Even though there were numerous people of all nationalities at the bar, we still found a table large enough to seat us. An all female Filipino band played both Asian and American music. We had almost instant service from a Malaysian waitress. I volunteered to buy the first round and ordered beers all around. In due course, the waitress brought the beer and gave me the bill. The beer was nearly eight dollars a glass and the glasses were only six ounces! I reached for my American Express card and quit buying rounds.

We didn't have too many more drinks before we decided to get back across the border. As the designated driver, I was at the wheel. We drove unimpeded through Bahrain's border guards and on across the bridge. Almost half way across we passed a sign that read: "All vehicles subject to search--the transportation of alcohol into the Kingdom is forbidden." Hackman, who was sitting in the passenger side seat, yelled, "Stop! Stop!" I slammed on the brakes and came to a stop in the far right lane. I knew no one had any alcohol so I couldn't imagine what had caused his excitement. "The ammo!" He said. "We've got all that damn ammo." There were two crates in the back of the Blazer that the Whackers had been using as benches. They got up and lifted the lids. The crates were full of enough guns and explosives to start a small war. "What in the hell are we going to do with it?" I asked him. "Let's dump the stuff in the Gulf!" Said Woody. "What the hell!" Hackman was fidgeting excitedly. He grabbed a grenade and sent it over the bridge. We listened for it hit the water. Then we started an assembly line from the car to the edge of the bridge. Grenades, mines, bullets, rocket launchers and flares, all went over the side. We all piled back in the truck and headed toward the Saudi check point.

"Let's freak'em out!" Said Hopi digging into an equipment box. He produced a hand full of chemical lights. Chemical lights or "chem-sticks" as we referred to them, consisted of a plastic tube about eight inches long, inside of which were chemicals and a small glass vile. Inside the glass vile were different chemicals. When the larger plastic tube was bent, the glass vile would break and the two chemicals would mix. The result was a very high intensity light. Hopi bent a chem-stick until the small glass vile broke. He then shook the chemicals until they glowed a bright green. With a pocket knife he cut-off the top of the chem-stick and poured the radiating contents all over his body. In an instant, he began to glow a bright, florescent green. All of the Whackers then broke open a chem-stick and doused themselves with the chemicals. They even doused Hackman and me in the front seat. Stoney got in on the act too. By the time we reached the Saudi border, the interior of the car was virtually light with our radiating bodies. The gate guards stared in disbelief as we pulled up to the gate. Seeing that we were Americans, however, they figured that it was safer to let us pass unchecked than to be contaminated by whatever it was that had infected us. They stood aside as we pulled through the border.

Over the next week I made three more trips to Bahrain. These trips were primarily to shop at the local souq. On my first shopping trip to Manamah with SFC Joe Franklin and Stoney, I found a thriving black market. I was able to buy Iraqi money, stamps and propaganda posters, all bearing Saddam Hussein's picture. They were big sellers at the PX.

I had planned a fourth trip to the Bahrain souq during the first week of April, when I received an emergency Red Cross message. My father had had a heart attack and was at that moment undergoing quadruple heart by-pass surgery in Los Angeles, CA. Within hours I had my gear packed and was standing on the tarmac at the Dhahran International Airport. Stoney and Hackman were with me. We had been through a lot over the past seven months and I knew that I would miss them. As much as I wanted to go home, it didn't seem right to be leaving them behind. We joked around for the last time.

Stoney and Hackman who had gone into the Airport PX while I was getting my orders validated, presented me with a T-shirt. Written in red lettering on a white shirt were the words "Mother of all Desert Rats!" We boasted that when we had arrived in November, Saddam Hussein had the fourth largest army in the world. Now, as I departed, he had only the second largest army in Iraq!

I promised Hackman and Stoney that I would call their families as soon as I got back. They escorted me onto a waiting C-5 cargo jet. Twenty-six hours later I arrived at Norton AFB, CA. I immediately went to see my father who was now satisfactorily recovering. As I sat in the hospital waiting room, I noticed the cover of *Sports Illustrated*. Nolan Ryan was beginning his twenty-fifth season as a professional baseball player. I vowed to see him pitch before the year was over. I wished Sammy, at the Dhahran International Hotel, could see him too. Three weeks later, I was discharged from the Army and the next week saw Nolan pitch the seventh no hitter of his career. He was forty-four years old.

Nearly half the unit trickled home over the next few months including Hackman. Finally, in the second week of July, the 826th Ordnance Company was deactivated and returned to reserve status. Stoney, Hackman and the other Vietnam veterans had finished their second oversees war tour. For me and most other Reservists around the country, our first tour was over. We went back to work to await the next call. . . ."By Order of the President of the United States of America you are hereby ordered to report. . . "

Captured Iraqi Frog-7 missile.

A camel wanders into The Badger Pit.

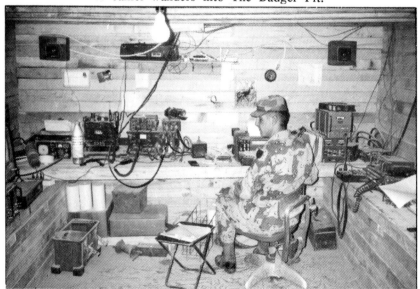

SPC Michael Anderson manning the underground communications bunker.

SFC David Schneider operates our heavy equipment.

LT crawls out from under an overturned Abrams M1A1
tank.

Kuwaiti Air Force plane in between missions.

SPC Frank Arado (Franco) and SPC Ralph Nachreiner
work on the 30 KW generator.

A post card from South St. Paul.

Khobar Towers was the largest American military holding center in Saudi Arabia.

The Service crew unloading equipment at the port.

Locals prepare a fresh goat for lunch.

SGT Clint Roberts, SPC Jeff Hole, SGT Roger Provenzano, SGT Perry Thew and SGT Ed Comstock in front of the Command Post.

SPC Kevin Webb, SPC Jeff Hole and SPC Scott Gennrich at the Port of Jabail.

Lt. Jeffrey J. Coonjohn

193

Abbreviations

1SG	First Sergeant
AAFES	Army & Air Force Exchange Service
APC	Armored Personnel Carrier
ARCENT	Army Central Command
ASG	Area Support Group
BDU	Battle Dress Uniform
BG	Brigadier General
Bn.	Battalion
C.O.	Company Commander
Co.	Company
Col.	Colonel
CPL	Corporal
CPT	Captain
CSC	Convoy Support Center
CSM	Command Sergeant Major
Gen.	General
Inf.	Infantry
JIB	Joint Information Bureau
KKMC	King Khalid Military City
KP	Kitchen Patrol
LOG Base	Logistical Base
Lt.	Lieutenant
LTC	Lieutenant Colonel
LTG	Lieutenant General
Main.	Maintenance
MAJ	Major
MG	Major General
MMC	Materiel Management Center
MP	Military Police
MRE	Meals Ready to Eat
MRO	Material Release Order
MSR	Main Supply Route
NCO	Non-Commissioned Officer
Ord.	Ordnance
PAO	Public Affairs Office
PFC	Private First Class

PVT	Private
PX	Post Exchange
R&R	Rest and Relaxation
S&S	Service and Support
S.R.	Saudi riyal
SFC	Sergeant First Class
SGT	Sergeant
SPC	Specialist
SSG	Staff Sergeant
Trans.	Transportation

ABOUT THE AUTHOR

• Jeffrey J. Coonjohn is an attorney by training, a soldier by choice and a writer by night. He was born and reared in Alaska's frontier where he cultivated a strong independence and creative ingenuity. He received his Bachelor of Arts degree from UCLA and his Doctor of Law degree from the University of Wisconsin. His military education includes JROTC training at Missouri Military Academy; Basic Training at Ft. Bliss, TX; Advanced Individual Training at Ft. Benjamin Harrison, IN; ROTC training at the University of Wisconsin; Advanced Officer Training at Ft. Lewis, WA; Army Airborne training at Ft. Benning, GA and Ordnance training at Red Stone Arsenal, AL.